PDM I
Piano for the Developing Musician

PDM I
Piano for the Developing Musician

Martha Hilley
The University of Texas at Austin

Lynn Freeman Olson
Composer and Consultant, New York City

West Publishing Company

St. Paul   New York   Los Angeles   San Francisco

Production Credits

Design and Composition: **David Whitten**

Music Engraving: **Korea Music Cooperators**

Cover Art: **The Metropolitan Museum of Art**, Purchase, 1967, Edward J. Kaufmann. Charitable Foundation Gift. (67,231.1-3)

Cover Design: **The Quarasan Group, Inc.**

We wish to thank the many publishers who were so kind to grant permission to reprint their works. Specific credit lines appear in the body of the text. **American Ballad** by Jeno Takacs, © Copyright 1981 by Universal Edition A.G., Wien. All rights reserved. Used by permission of European American Music Distributors Corporation, sole U.S. Agent for Universal Edition.

Printed in the United States of America

Library of Congress Cataloging in Publication Data

Hilley, Martha.
  Piano for the developing musician.
1. Piano—Instruction and study. 2. Harmony, Keyboard.
I. Olson, Lynn Freeman. II. Title.
MT 220.H56 1985   786.3'041   84-19550
ISBN 0-314-85247-6 (v. 1)
ISBN 0-314-87394-5 (v. 2)

Contents

1. Intervals

2. Pentascales

3. Root Position Triads

4. Extended Use of Intervals, Pentascales and Triads/Dominant Seventh

5. Chord Shapes / Pentascales With Black-Key Groups

Musical Evaluation Chapter

8. White-Key Minor Scale Fingerings Diatonic Harmonies in Minor

9. Secondary Dominants/ Styles of Accompanying

10. Melodic Ornamentation

Preface

Piano for the Developing Musician, in contrast to many other keyboard texts, was researched and created for a highly specific population: the college music major who must demonstrate a variety of musical skill areas at the piano.

PDM does not pamper the student. The text moves quickly but thoroughly in areas where general musical knowledge exists; it moves more gradually in areas where technique needs development. It has been demonstrated time and again that when expectations are low, student achievement will be low; when expectations are higher, and the means for acquiring the requisite skills are delineated, student achievement will be far higher.

The key is understanding. The text features inquiry and activities designed to illumine the keyboard reality of music theory. The primary discoveries in the text grow out of piano literature itself. We are teaching music, and the need to produce that music with understanding should generate the related skills and extensions. Practicality is not ignored, for such aspects as harmonization, elementary score reading, scale and chord facility, and transposition are developed step by step.

The chapters in PDM are full. They were not necessarily designed to be completed within specific time frames; they are simply organized progressively by subject. The range of skill areas, however, is complete.

The Rhythm Cassette (▣) is a unique feature of each PDM book. High quality percussion performances have been arranged and specially recorded with narration to accompany selected activities in the text. A small cassette symbol in the text indicates that a coordinated sound sequence will be found on the Rhythm Cassette. The cassette lends momentum, enriches the total sound, and coaxes steadiness out of the student with vibrant rhythm. The cassette should be used for independent practice but may also serve as a useful class tool.

Each chapter in PDM is divided into the following sections:

EXEMPLARY REPERTOIRE
Discoveries are based on this literature, and steps for learning are provided. A full historical range is covered.

TOPICS TO EXPLORE AND DISCUSS
Selected names and terms are suggested. Elaboration appears in the Teacher's Manual for your convenience.

RELATED SKILLS AND ACTIVITIES
Technique—A series of drills and etudes stresses finger and hand development, independence, and coordination.
Reading—The challenge of reading and sight-playing music that uses the entire keyboard is presented regularly. Many styles and keys are involved, as are a variety of score configurations and clefs.
Keyboard Theory—Drills and exercises stress full understanding of the subject matter.
Harmonization—Melodies from folk and composed sources are presented for accompanying in a variety of styles.
Transposition—This musicianly skill is stressed through regular assignments, always based on theoretical understanding.
Improvisation—The ability to express oneself freely at the keyboard grows through assignments based on the acquired technical and theoretical skills.
Ensemble—There is an equal emphasis on duet repertoire and multikeyboard scores, both original and transcribed.
Composition—Brief assignments are based on repertoire as well as theory.

SUBSEQUENT REPERTOIRE
Additional selections of keyboard literature appear, often with brief study aids.

We are both practitioners of what might be termed a "humanistic" approach to music teaching. In this text you will find that we stress those aspects of music that do not change—its expressive nature, its freedom within organization, its social nature, and its eclectic qualities—all applied to the individual as a unique music maker. These things we teach, and we happen to be teaching them through the piano keyboard.

Acknowledgments

Had anyone told us that our seedlings would not only grow to become awesome trees but would also develop their own complex ecosystem, we might have reconsidered this project. But PDM needed to be written, and so the project took up residence in our lives. Somehow, each door we open leads to another, and neither of us is known to be reluctant to explore. So, we found ourselves spending long, long hours in recording studios, music libraries, museums, offices, conference rooms, borrowed apartments and houses, airports, and the like. We conferred in the mountains of Italy and in student lunchrooms, in friendly Brussels restaurants and on dusty lanes in a small Texas town. We became major factors in the financial success of several airlines, telephone companies, delivery services, and stationery stores. We were tired, but we loved it. Now we have so many to thank for their help and guidance. Our editor, Clark Baxter, calms our world with confident smiles, and his commitment to our project is total. His wonderful wife, Abigail Sterne Baxter, is our editorial consultant and great friend. Our talented production editor, Lenore Franzen, is expertise itself and keeps us in line. The staff and sales force of West Publishing Company are unfailingly friendly and enthusiastic. James Schnars was our accurate, patient, and helpful assistant in acquiring permissions and organizing the New York work site. Rose Schreibel masterminded the Teacher's Manual production in New York and generated the indexes. David Whitten and his assistant Carolyn Falletta were the swift and expert design artists. Special thanks to David's wife Monika for her meticulous help with mechanicals.

We wish to thank those who read the text and offered many helpful suggestions: Richard Anderson, Brigham Young University; Charlene Cox, Wichita State University; Jerry Davidson, Kent State University; Dolores Johnson, SUNY, Potsdam; Marguerite Miller; Larry Rast, Northern Illinois University; Joan Reist, University of Nebraska, Lincoln.

In Austin, the books were test-taught thoroughly, and we want to thank those graduate teaching assistants and their students who not only put up with less-than-perfect copies and frequent changes but also offered many useful suggestions.

Our audio production team was stellar. Robert Fedson, percussionist, brought his marvelous skill and creativity to each highly involved recording session. Bill Conner, our gifted audio engineer and supervisor, treated each sound with love and dedication, and his calm, professional approach was a daily marvel. Our narrator and end-of-line producer was Dr. Merrill Staton who combines his musical expertise with skill in audio production.

For special advice and support we wish to thank Dr. Hunter March, Dr. Dorothy Payne, J. Theodore Prochazka, and the editors of Silver Burdett Music. For specially composed music we must thank Ruth Schonthal, Susan Ogilvy, and Joseph M. Martin.

Martha Hilley

Lynn Freeman Olson

PIANO FOR THE DEVELOPING MUSICIAN assumes previous musical knowledge. Not every music major, however, has rudimentary piano skills. To make it possible to begin Chapter 1 in a class setting, we offer here some ''entrance level'' expectations. Following these, beginning piano reading is given a rapid review. For those who may wish some further aid, we suggest these brief beginner texts.

Olson: RIGHT FROM THE START (Carl Fischer)
Stecher, et al: LEARNING TO PLAY (G. Schirmer)

Assumptions:

READING

- Pitch names on the grand staff
- Functions of ♯, ♭, ♮, x, ♭♭

RHYTHM

- Common meter signatures, notes, and rest values
- Common tempo indications

MUSICIANSHIP

- Common dynamic indications
- Common phrasing and articulation marks
- Basic awareness of musical shape and motion
- Major key signatures and their functions

Rapid Guide:
Reading Music at the Piano

In piano music, fingers are numbered.

5 4 3 2 1   1 2 3 4 5

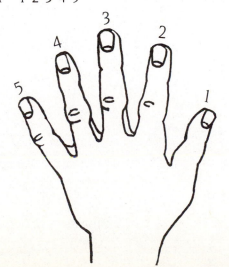
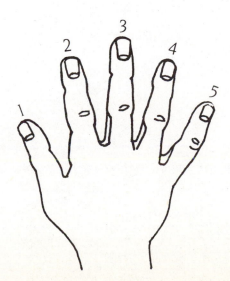

Unless otherwise indicated, when two staves are joined, notes on the upper staff are for right hand (RH) and notes on the lower staff are for left hand (LH).

We relate the grand staff to the piano keyboard.

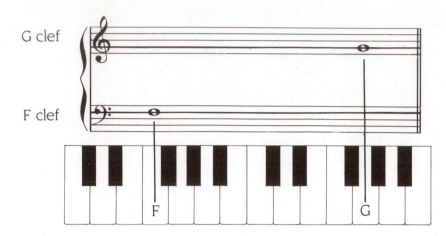

G clef

F clef

F   G

Play.

mf

Play these blocked intervals that use G and F.

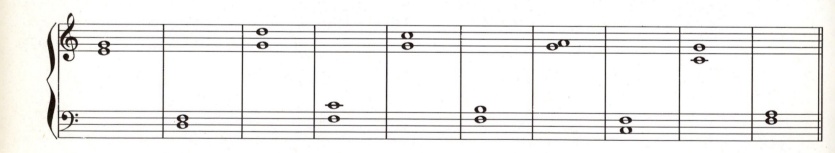

Play. What finger combination *could* you use?

Easily

mp

Locate the following.

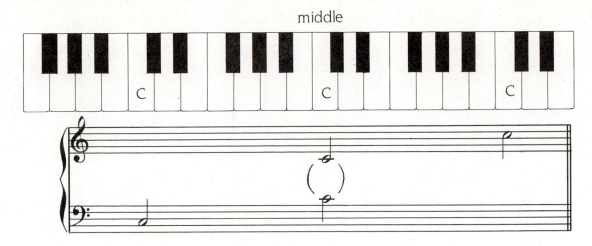

Plan fingering and play.

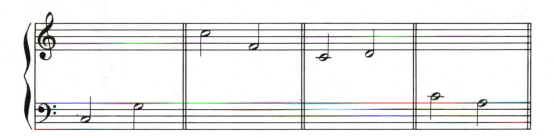

Plan fingering and play.

Name each blocked interval, plan fingering, and play.

Block the intervals. Play as written.

Locate the following.

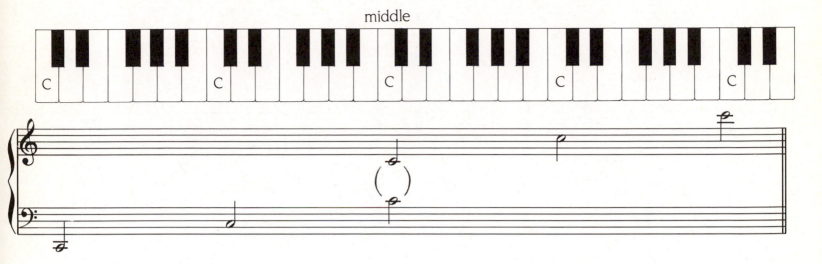

Plan fingering and play.

Play hands together.

When reading a score, for the first time or later, try to realize music on the keyboard as much as possible without looking down at the keys.

Feel two black keys; locate and play each example.

Feel three black keys; locate and play each example.

Reading music at the piano is much easier if you scan the score in *groups* of notes instead of one note at a time, especially in terms of hand position and logical fingering.

What would be logical fingering? Play.

Key signatures can be viewed as lists of flats or sharps occurring throughout the example, section, or composition and affecting all notes of the same name no matter where they appear on the staff.

Key signatures, of course, are much more than lists; they help summarize and remind us of tonalities.

- In major sharp signatures, the last sharp (farthest to the right) is a half step below the *key name*.

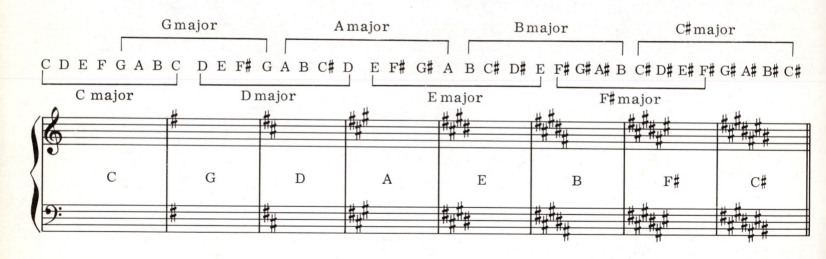

- In major flat signatures, the next-to-last flat names the key (F major has one flat).

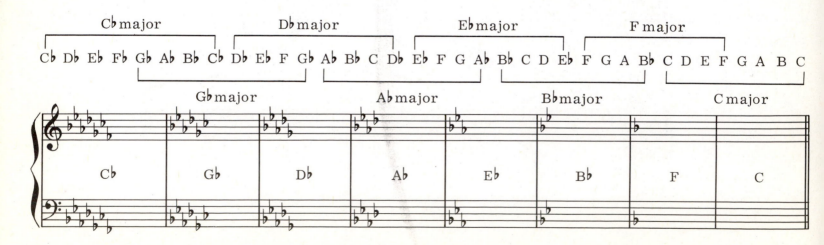

Play

Key of _____

Eagerly

Key of _____

Andante cantabile

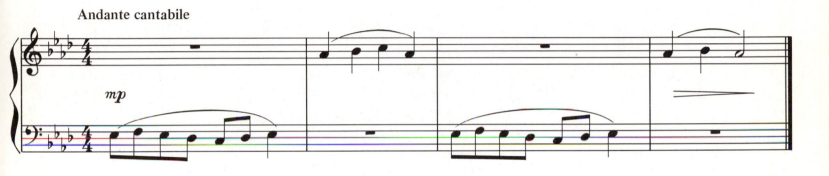

Key of _____

Con spirito

Key of _____

Andantino

1.

Intervals

EXEMPLARY REPERTOIRE **One Four Seven** Lynn Freeman Olson

INQUIRY

    1. Scan the piece. Observe:

        • actual number of measures to be learned
        • pattern of intervallic change

    2. Determine logical fingering.

    3. Given the meter, determine a tempo.

    4. Given the overall character, determine dynamics.

    5. What does the title mean?

PERFORMANCE

    1. Block the right- and left-hand intervals, hands together, restriking only when intervals change.

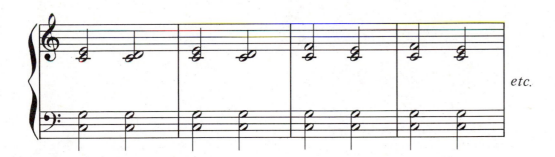

    2. With both hands, tap the rhythms of the piece on top of the piano.

    3. Play right-hand intervals while tapping left-hand rhythms on top of the piano.

    4. Play as written.

One Four Seven

LYNN FREEMAN OLSON

1

TOPICS TO EXPLORE AND DISCUSS

- Alternating meters *versus* variable meters
- Intervals: melodic and harmonic

RELATED SKILLS AND ACTIVITIES

TECHNIQUE

The following exercises use harmonic and melodic intervals. Determine a logical fingering for each example before playing.

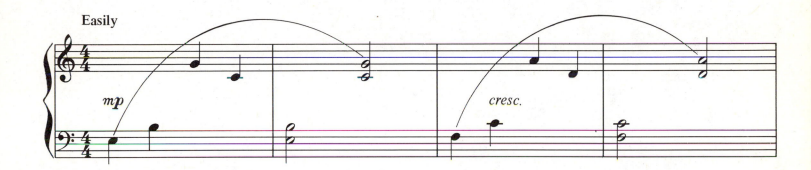

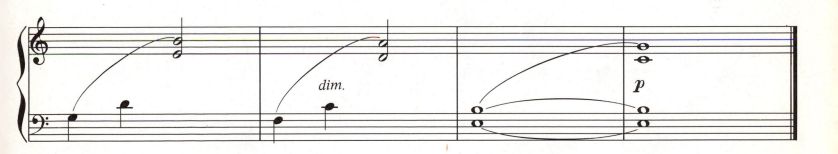

Alla marcia

LH

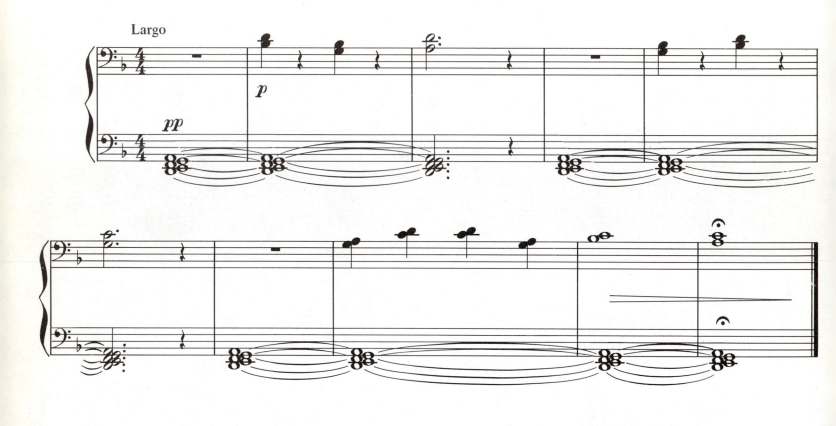

Largo

Sturdily

RH

1

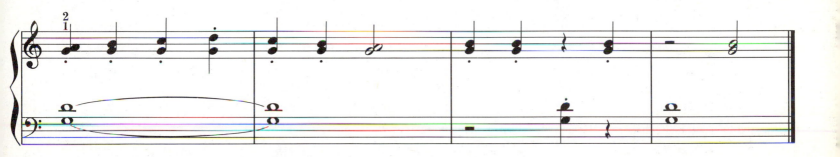

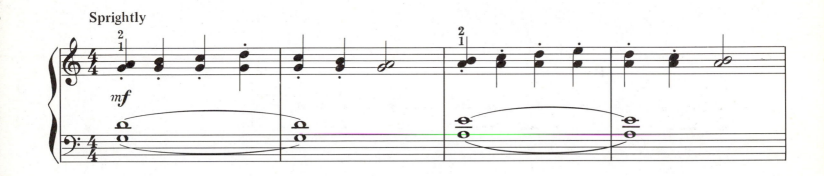

READING

1. *Intervallic reading.* With hand in lap, think

- interval
- keyboard location
- fingering

Then play.

The Rhythm Cassette will dictate a drill based on the preceding intervals.

8

2. *Rhythmic reading.* Tap the following while counting the beat.

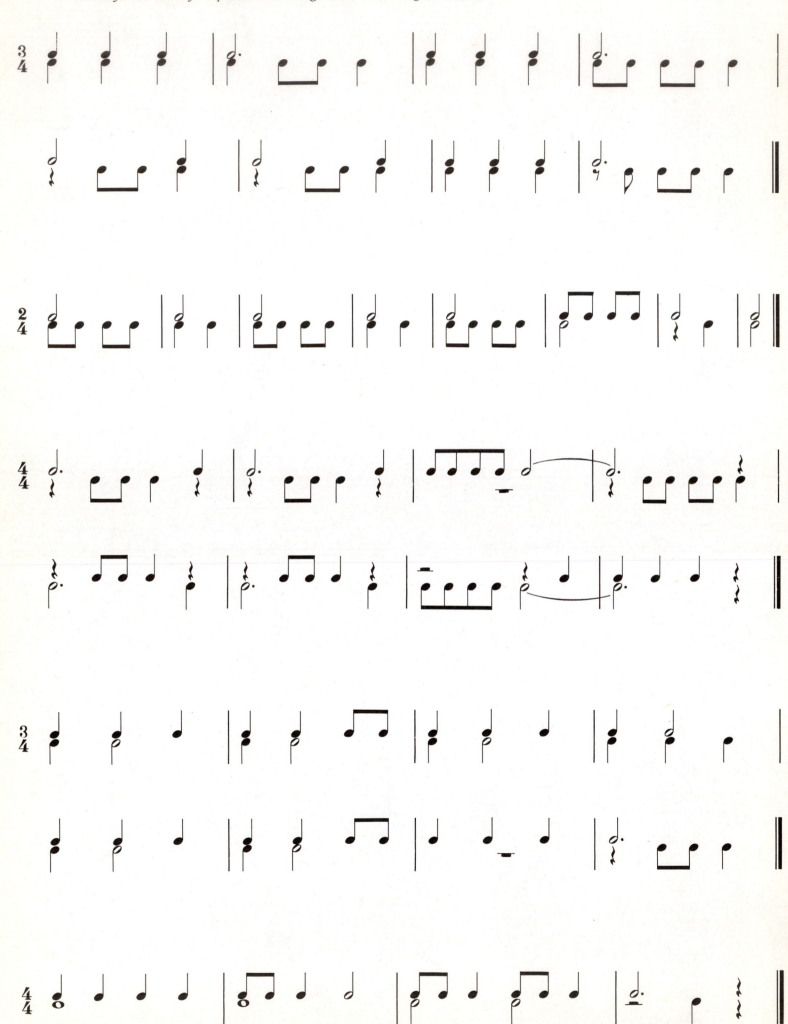

KEYBOARD THEORY

The Rhythm Cassette will call for various intervals to be played above and below the following pitches. Use white keys only.

Rewind the Rhythm Cassette to 1-2 and play the designated intervals above and below the following pitches.

HARMONIZATION

Harmonize each of the following melodies with the fifth indicated in parentheses. Play the fifth blocked (in long or short values) and/or broken. Select an accompaniment style to enhance the mood.

Happily   American

Simply   British

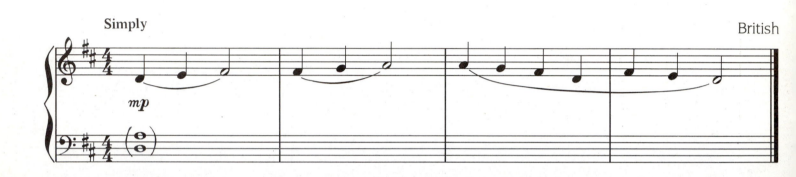

Dreamily   American

Lively · American

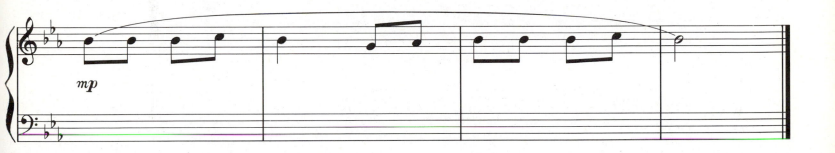

TRANSPOSITION

Play *One Four Seven* with the first interval based on G, transposing the rest of the piece accordingly.

IMPROVISATION

1-3

Improvise melodically, using the prescribed harmonic and melodic intervals. The intervals will change every eight bars.

ENSEMBLE

The following is a "spoken invention." Discuss as a class the musical meaning of the word *invention*. Perform as a three-part chant with clapping. Additional directions follow the score.

My Dog Treed a Rabbit

American
Arranged by Lynn Freeman Olson

Improvise on black keys to match the rhythm. "Rabbit" is always played on E♭ and G♭.
Clapping part plays a bass ostinato throughout.

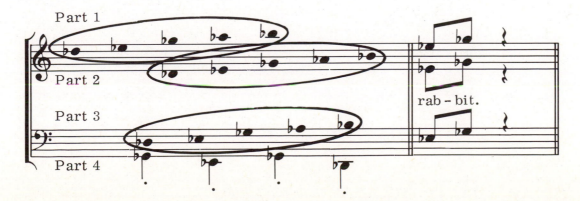

Hoo Doo
(In a Hollywood Bazaar)

LYNN FREEMAN OLSON

image

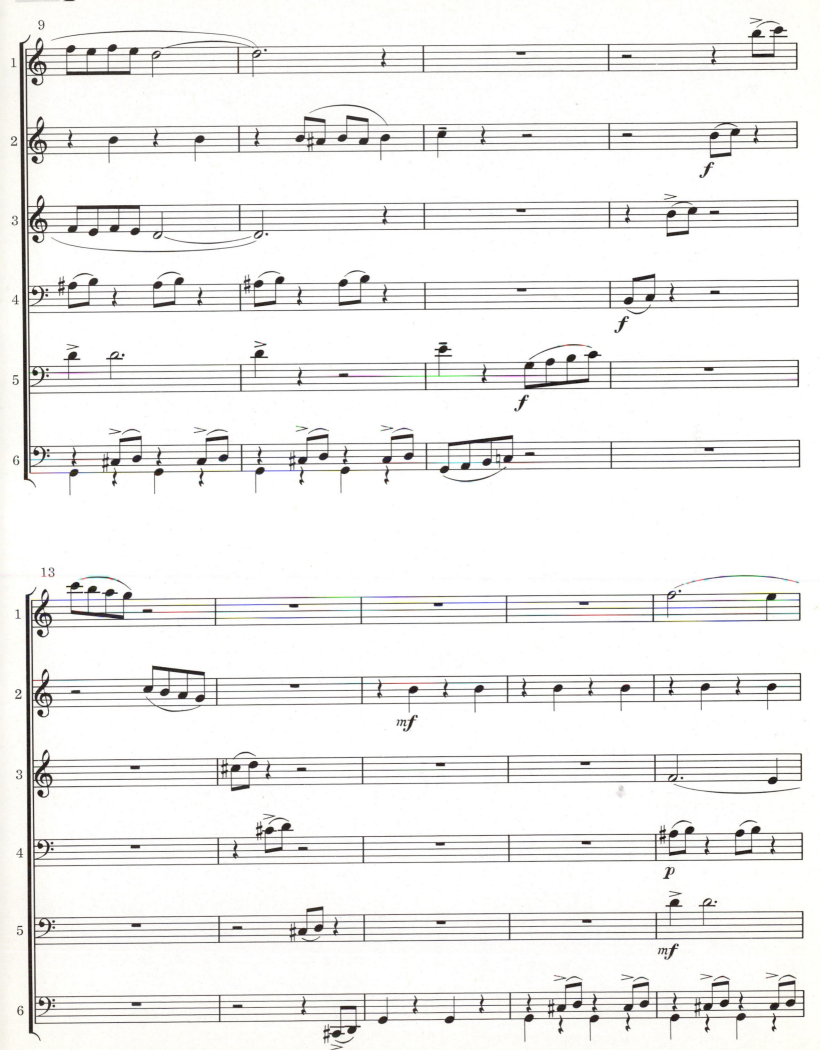

COMPOSITION

Create a piece in the style of *One Four Seven* using variable meter. Refer to observations in Inquiry section (page 3).

SUBSEQUENT REPERTOIRE

Define the term *syncopation*. Listen carefully for balance in the two voices. Plan fingering for the position shifts.

Syncopation

DANIEL GOTTLOB TÜRK
(1756-1813)

Seaview, After Turner uses fifths and tone clusters that cover the span of a fifth. Determine the pattern of motion throughout the piece from one position to another. What did you discover?

Notice the sign for pedal.

down   *hold*   *up*

Seaview, After Turner

LYNN FREEMAN OLSON

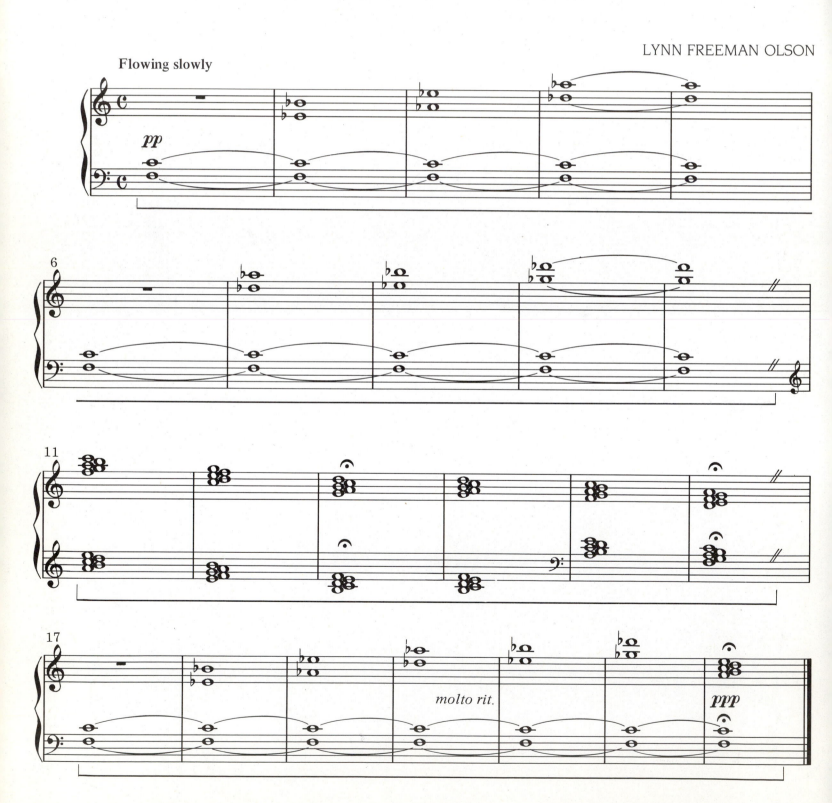

Block each interval position in *Saturday Smile*, keeping a steady beat.

etc.

Experiment to find a tempo that feels right for the piece. Then perform as written.

Saturday Smile

LYNN FREEMAN OLSON

2.

Pentascales

EXEMPLARY REPERTOIRE   **Legato Study** Béla Bartók

INQUIRY

   1. Scan the piece. Observe:

- type of motion between hands
- melodic direction
- melodic range

      A pentascale is a pattern of five consecutive stepwise pitches.
      Name the pitches of the pentascale used in *Legato Study*.

- sequence
- phrase structure

   2. Determine logical fingering.

PERFORMANCE

   1. A *legato* sound is appropriate. Lift hands at the end of each phrase to prepare for the next one.

   2. Use dynamic shading to emphasize the phrase structure.

   3. Sing and shape in the air, then play again as written.

Legato Study

from *The First Term at the Piano*

BELA BARTOK
(1881-1945)

TOPICS TO EXPLORE AND DISCUSS

- Sound: Describe the musical effects of parallel, contrary, and oblique motion.
  Describe the musical effect of one octave *versus* two octaves apart. What is the visual effect?
- Effect of three-measure phrases
- Béla Bartók

RELATED SKILLS AND ACTIVITIES

TECHNIQUE

1. The pentascale used in the Bartók *Legato Study* is major.

All major pentascales use the same pattern of whole and half steps.

Perform the following major pentascale phrases.

and so on, upward, on every white-key major pentascale pattern.

and so on, downward, on every white-key major pentascale pattern.

Repeat:

- finger staccato, *mp*
- wrist staccato, *f*

2. Play the fifth. Feel shoulder, elbow, and wrist relax; then play the other notes with finger staccato.

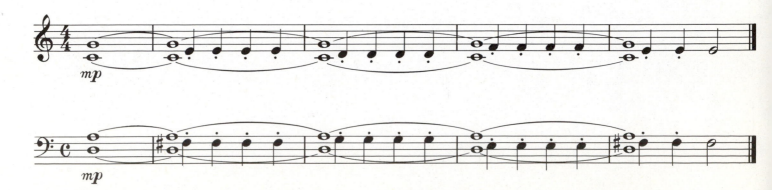

3. *One-handed exercises*: Play with the nondominant hand; tap the beat with the other hand.

Not fast   Spiritual

With energy   Canadian

Tap downbeats with the other hand.

Tap 𝅘𝅥𝅭 beats with the other hand.

READING

2-1

1. Number the phrases of the Bartók *Legato Study* (page 21).
   Play random phrases as directed by the Rhythm Cassette.

2-2

2. Play the following unison melodies using Rhythm Cassette background. Two tempos
   are used for each example. Consider:

   • evenness of touch
   • phrasing
   • dynamics

KEYBOARD THEORY

1. Play major pentascales beginning on each white key (C, D, E, G, A, B). Name the pitches as you play. *Pentascales use consecutive letter names.*

2. In a major pentascale, the bottom tone is called *tonic* (I) and the top tone is called *dominant* (V). Pentascale melodies may be accompanied by these single tones.

   Generally, when the melody is made mostly of tones 1, 3, and 5, accompany with tonic (I); when mostly of 2 and 4, accompany with dominant (V). Your ear will always be the final test of appropriate accompaniment.

For right-hand melodies, you may choose to place the left hand in pentascale position as illustrated. We also encourage the frequent use of dominant *below* tonic. This is easy when you place your left-hand thumb on a white-key tonic.

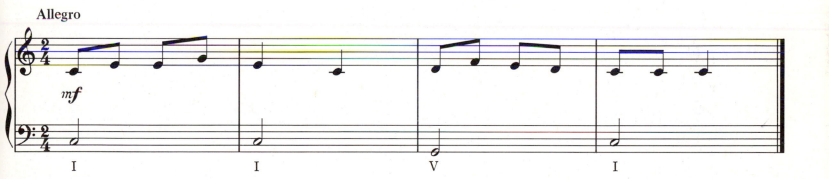

HARMONIZATION

Accompany the following melodies with tonic and dominant tones. Try both the ''dominant above'' and ''dominant below'' left-hand positions.

FRANZ JOSEPH HAYDN
(1732-1809)

TRANSPOSITION

2-3

1. Transpose each melody and accompaniment in Harmonization section to two other major pentascales.

2. Transpose each example in Reading section as directed by the Rhythm Cassette.

3. Transpose the following to C, F, and E majors.

Quiet Conversation

LYNN FREEMAN OLSON

IMPROVISATION

2-4

Improvise melodically within a major pentascale to a rhythmic pattern as directed by the Rhythm Cassette.

ENSEMBLE

1. Create the following ensemble.

   - One group of players performs the upper voice of the Bartók *Legato Study* as written.
   - Another group transposes this voice to G major, beginning *down a fourth*.
   - Play together twice; on second time, switch parts.

   The resulting sound resembles a feature of *parallel organum*, a type of polyphony common in the ninth and tenth centuries.

2. Perform the following "spoken invention" as directed below. Chant and *patsch* (produce a sound by slapping the outer thigh with an open hand).

Hoosen Johnny

American Chant
Arranged by Lynn Freeman Olson

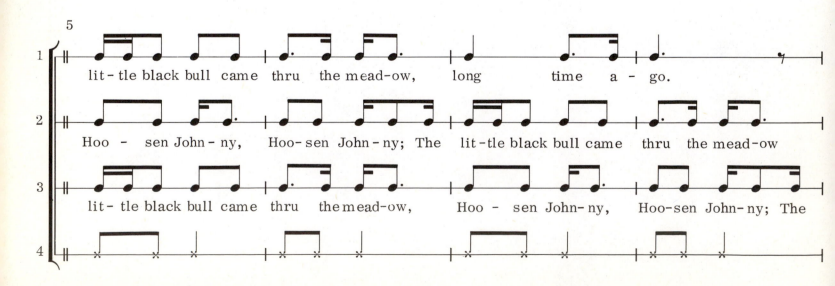

3. Improvise a keyboard ensemble to match the rhythm of *Hoosen Johnny*.

Part 1

Part 2

Part 3

Part 4

Players 1, 2, and 3 create, and agree on, a single melodic fragment to play each time for

Long time a - go.

4. Dynamics have been omitted. Plan "echo" effects. (What about bar 17?) Choose a partner and play.

Fanfare
from *Notebook for Wolfgang*

LEOPOLD MOZART
(1719-1787)
Adapted by Lynn Freeman Olson

2
COMPOSITION

Based on the principle of strict *parallel organum*, create a 12-measure composition using major pentascales that begin on white keys.

SUBSEQUENT REPERTOIRE

Echoing employs imitation. Where in the piece does exact imitation cease?

Echoing

LOUIS KÖHLER, Op. 218
(1820-1886)

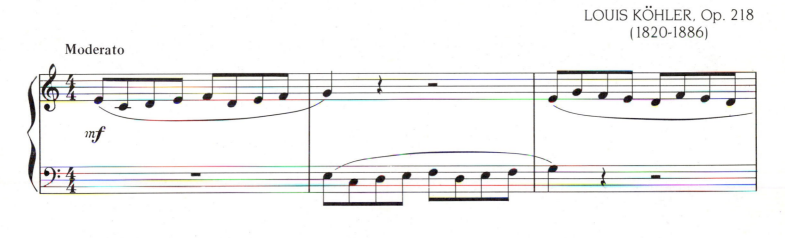

The Bartók *Study* uses two pentascales. Compare the two keyboard placements. How is the sound affected?

This is a three-part form with coda. Where does the coda begin?

Study: Changing Hand Position
from *The First Term at the Piano*

BÉLA BARTÓK
(1881-1945)

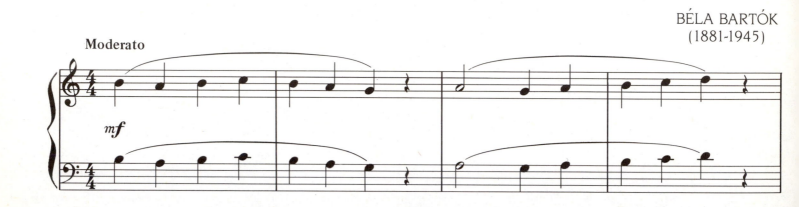

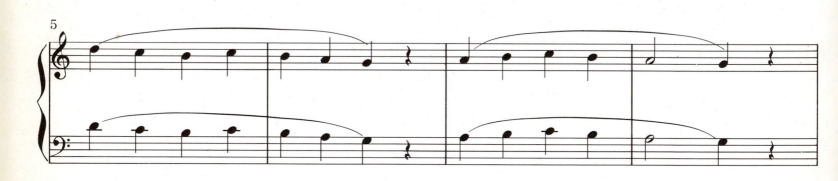

2

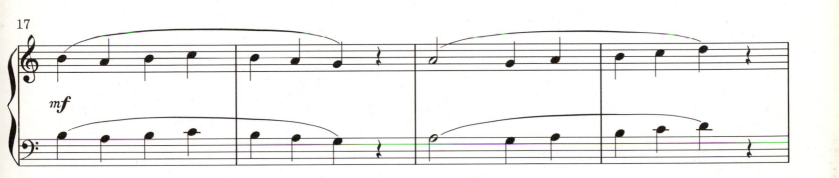

Questioning uses primarily melodic thirds. Play each third as a solid harmonic interval using the indicated fingering. Then play the piece as written.

Questioning

JOHN LA MONTAINE
(1920-   )

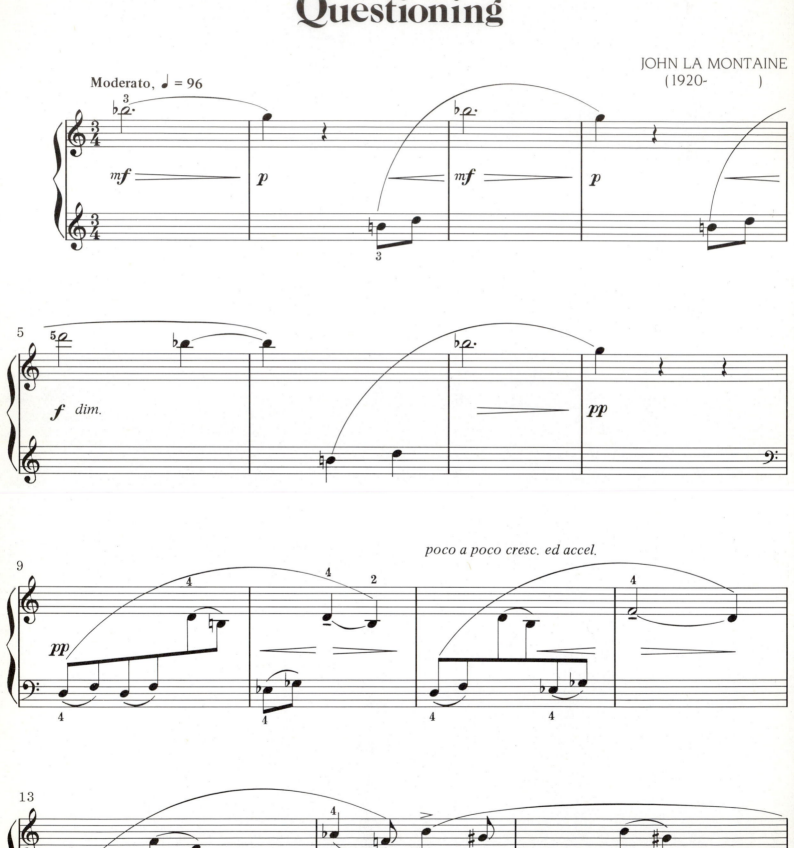

2

Tempo I

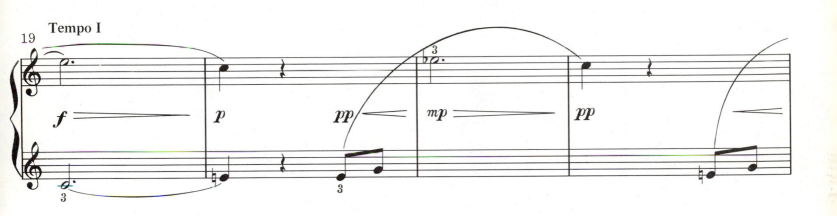

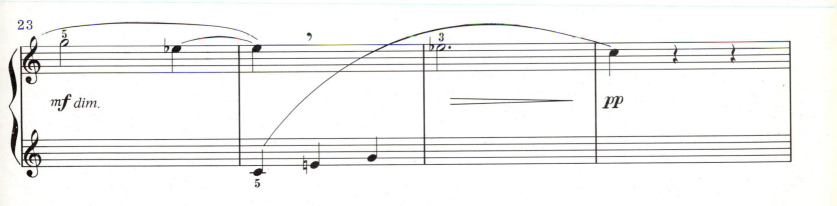

Study *Allegro in* C. Discuss the dynamics of the B section. Shape phrases in the air with left hand as you play right hand. Play as written.

Allegro in C

ALEXANDER REINAGLE
(1756-1809)

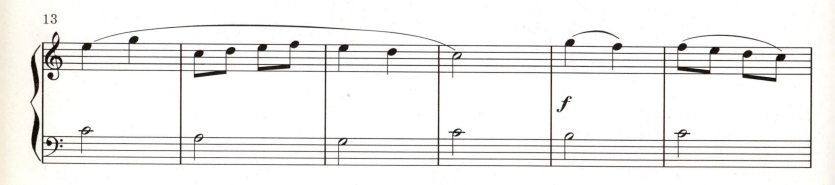

D.C. al Fine

2 Improvise on all boxed pitches in *Inner View.*

Inner View

LYNN FREEMAN OLSON

3.

Root Position Triads

EXEMPLARY REPERTOIRE   **Scherzo**, Op. 39, No. 12 Dmitri Kabalevsky

INQUIRY

1. Scan the piece. Observe:

    • repetitious shapes and their relationships
    • sequential patterns and direction

    Tones 1, 3, and 5 of a pentascale form a triad.
    The tones of a triad may be played singly or in various groupings.

    • hand position shifts
    • contrasting articulations
    • unity and variety

2. Determine logical fingering.

PERFORMANCE

1. Play hands together as blocked triads with two pulses to each position.

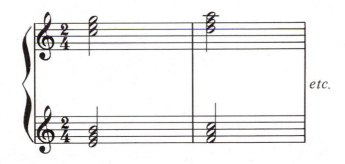

2. Play as written.

Scherzo
from 24 *Pieces for Children*

DMITRI KABALEVSKY, Op. 39, No. 12
(1904-   )

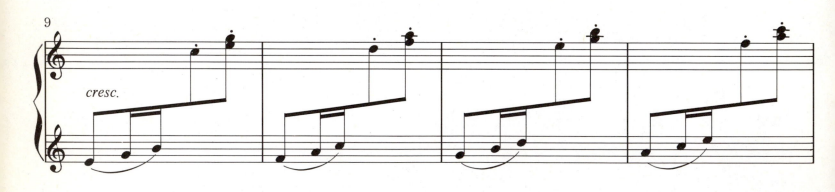

TOPICS TO EXPLORE AND DISCUSS

- Dmitri Kabalevsky: Identify several musical contemporaries.
- Vincent Persichetti

RELATED SKILLS AND ACTIVITIES

TECHNIQUE

1. Play.

2. Repeat the preceding exercises using two hands.

3. Play blocked triads built on the right-hand melodic tones of the Bartók *Legato Study* (page 21).

3

4. Play with the indicated hand; conduct with the other.

5. Play.

READING

3-1

1. *Rhythmic reading*: The percussionist demonstrates the following patterns on the Rhythm Cassette. Each pattern is heard twice.

• First time: Count the beat aloud as you listen.
• Second time: Tap the pattern while counting the beat.

3

The percussionist will demonstrate the *lower* voice of the following patterns. You will hear each two times.

- First time: Count the beat aloud.
- Second time: Tap the *upper* pattern while counting the beat.

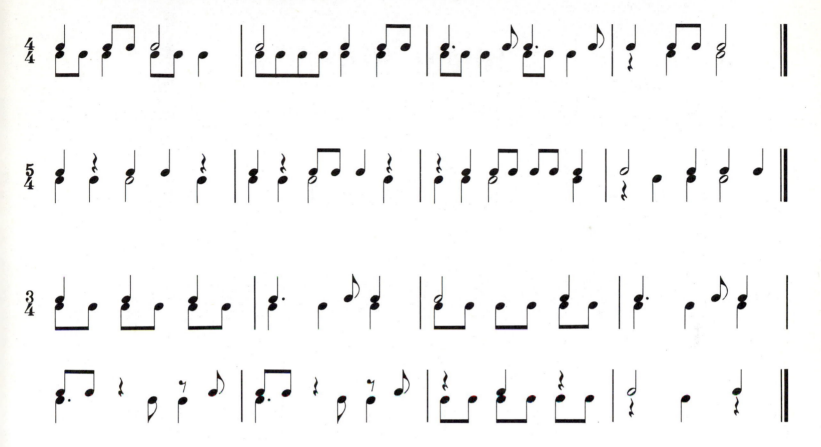

Tap the following rhythms while counting the beat. (There is no Rhythm Cassette demonstration with this exercise.)

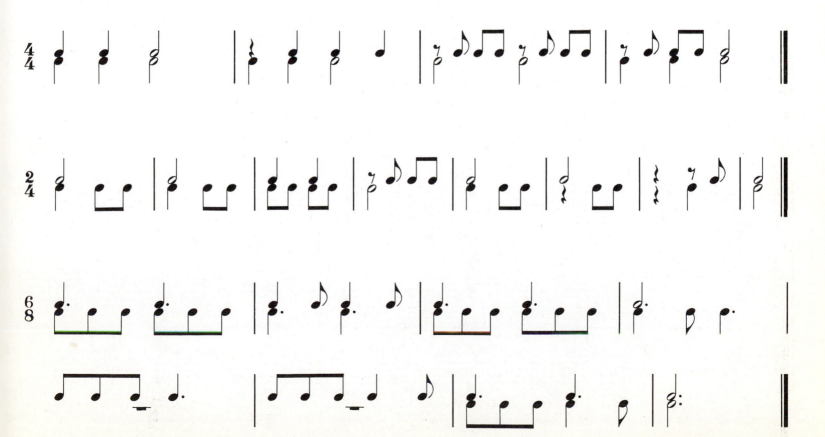

44

2. Perform *Silent Stars* as a three-part keyboard ensemble, each player realizing just one part. Sing the part you are playing. Each student should then rehearse playing pairs of parts simultaneously.

- Alto and Soprano 2
- Soprano 2 and Soprano 1
- Alto and Soprano 1

Silent Stars

LYNN FREEMAN OLSON

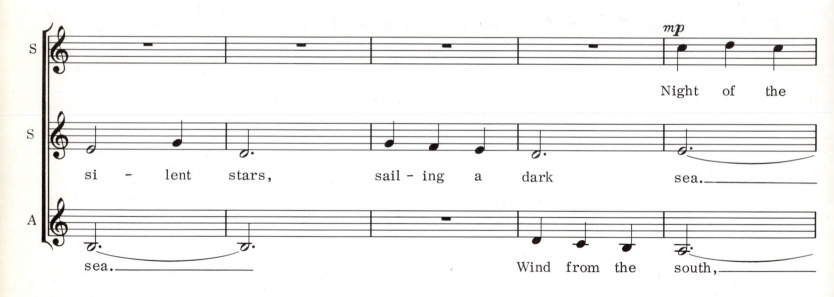

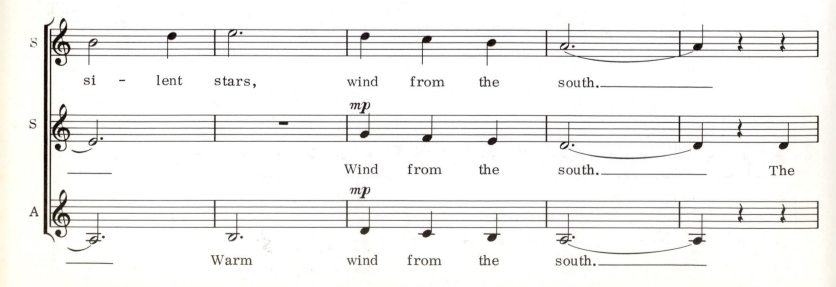

3

Eyes of night, they do not guide___ us.___

eyes of night, they stare, they do not guide___ us.___

Eyes_____ do not guide___ us,___

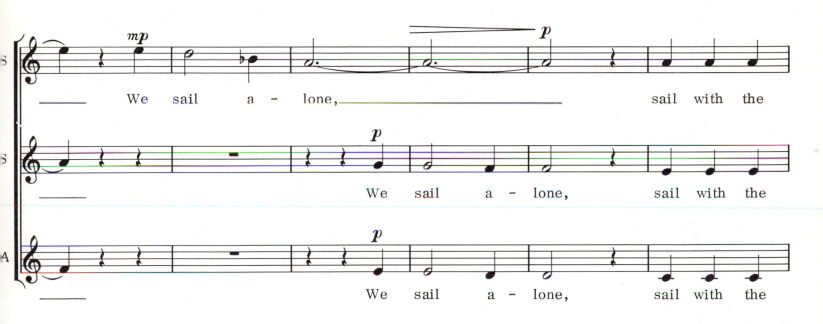

_____ We sail a - lone,_____ sail with the

_____ We sail a - lone, sail with the

_____ We sail a - lone, sail with the

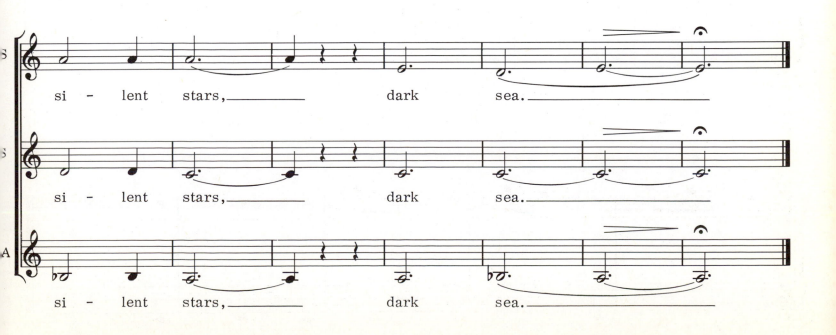

si - lent stars,___ dark sea.___

si - lent stars,___ dark sea.___

si - lent stars,___ dark sea.___

3. Block each shape in the Gurlitt *Allegretto* to demonstrate the harmonic rhythm.
   Keep a steady beat.

etc.

Play as written.

Allegretto

CORNELIUS GURLITT, Op. 117, No. 5
(1820-1901)

3

4. Play as written.

Minuetto

ALEXANDER REINAGLE
(1756-1809)

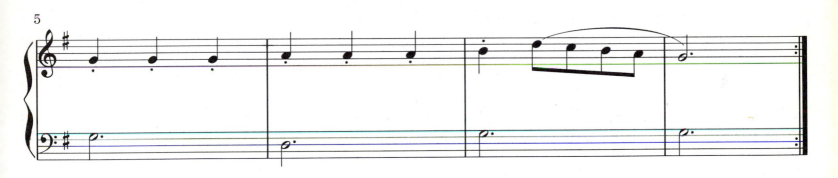

KEYBOARD THEORY

1. Play triads in the left hand built on each tone of the C major pentascale. Determine the quality of each triad (major or minor) and assign a Roman numeral to it.

2. Play triads in the left hand built on each triad of the following major pentascales:

   D,   E,   F,   G,   A

   Play triads in the right hand built on each triad of the following major pentascales:

   D,   E,   F,   G,   A

3. Play triads hands together as directed on the Rhythm Cassette.

3-3

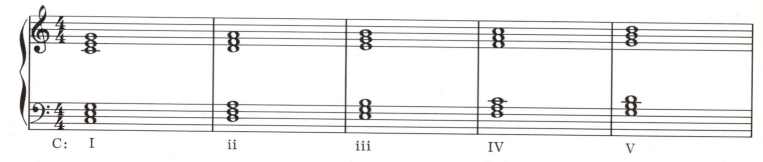

C: I   ii   iii   IV   V

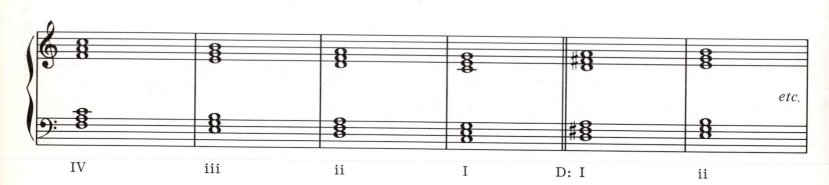

IV   iii   ii   I   D: I   ii

4. Play the same pentascale triads rhythmically in $\frac{6}{8}$, two measures to a triad—one measure broken, hand-to-hand, followed by one measure blocked, hand-to-hand.

C: I   I   ii

5. Play the pentascale triads I and V in the major keys indicated. Follow the example.

C: I   V   I   I   V   I   D: I   V   I   I   V   I   etc.

Play in C, D, E, F, G, A major.

HARMONIZATION

1. Refer to the melodies on pages 25-26. Harmonize with triads instead of single tones.

2. When deciding harmonies to be used, consider the chord tones in the melody. Realize that for any single tones there are three triadic possibilities; for two chord tones, two possibilities.

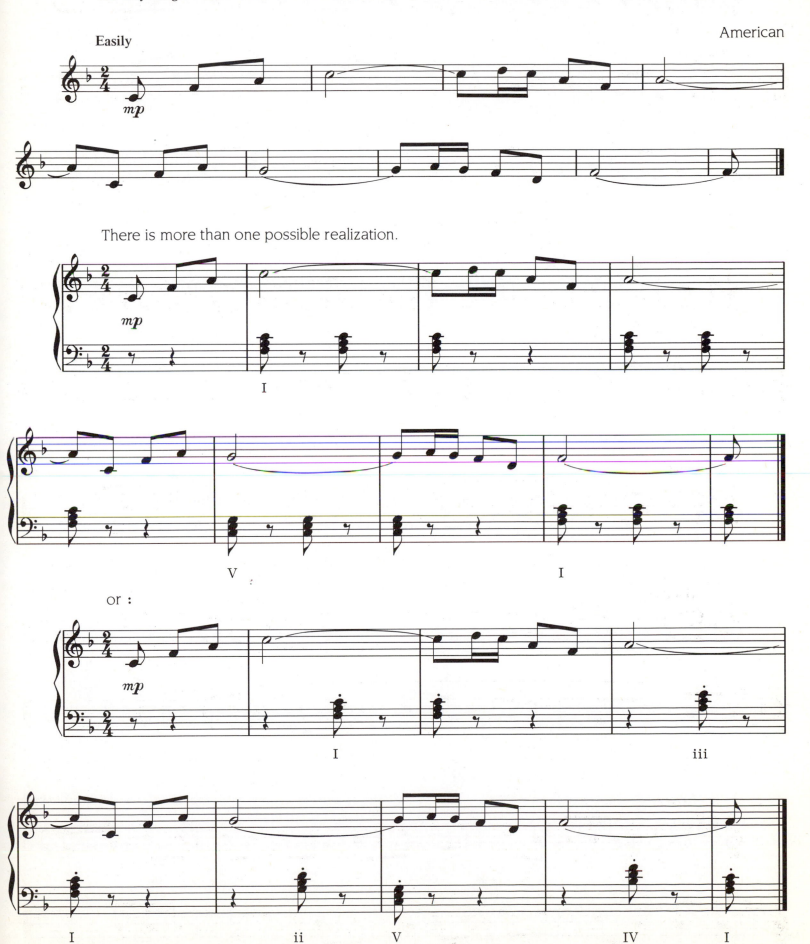

3. Choose from I, ii, iii, IV, and V and harmonize the following melodies.

4. Return once more to the melodies on pages 25-26. Harmonize with a two-handed accompaniment while singing the melody.

Example:

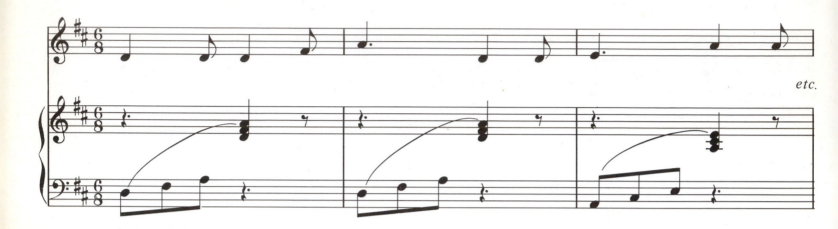

etc.

TRANSPOSITION

1. Transpose *Echoing* (page 31) to all white-key major pentascales.

2. Transpose *Lullaby* to C, D, F, and A majors.

Lullaby

LYNN FREEMAN OLSON

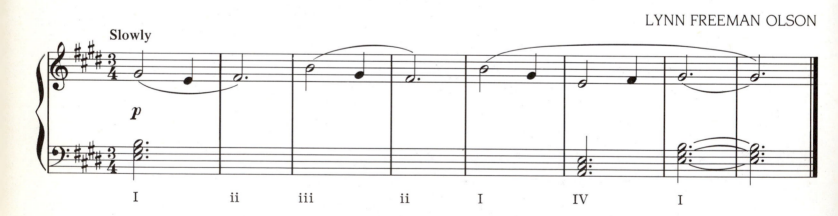

Slowly

p

I   ii   iii   ii   I   IV   I

Play again in transposed keys, this time using a broken chord accompaniment.

etc.

I   ii

3. Divide players for a two-part round (second entry at *) and play the following melody.

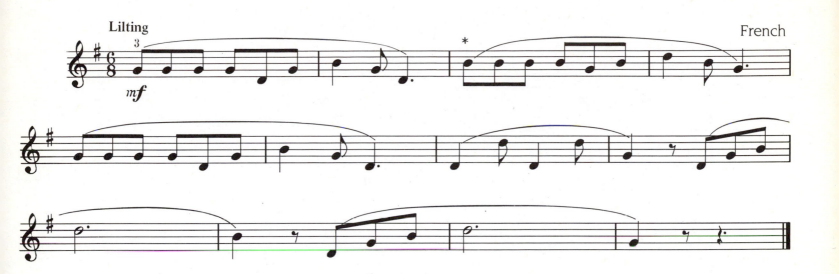

Transpose to F, A, and B majors in unison and as a round.

4. Transpose the *Minuetto* by Reinagle (page 47) to A and E major.

IMPROVISATION

3-4

1. Play the following triad progression hands together. Use the keys of D major, F major, and A major. Using the Rhythm Cassette, play:

$\frac{4}{4}$ I | IV | ii | V | iii | ii | V | I   ‖

2. Play the same progressions as two-handed accompaniments.

3. Improvise a right-hand melody consisting of *chord tones only*. This may be done as a "round robin" activity in class: All students play solid whole-note triads in the left hand until their turn comes for melodic improvisation.

ENSEMBLE

1. Play *Country Dance* six times, moving to the next part down each time (Part 6 moves to Part 1).

- First time, *p*
- Second time, *mp*
- Third time, *mf*
- Fourth time, *f*
- Fifth time, *p*
- Sixth time, *pp*

Country Dance

LYNN FREEMAN OLSON

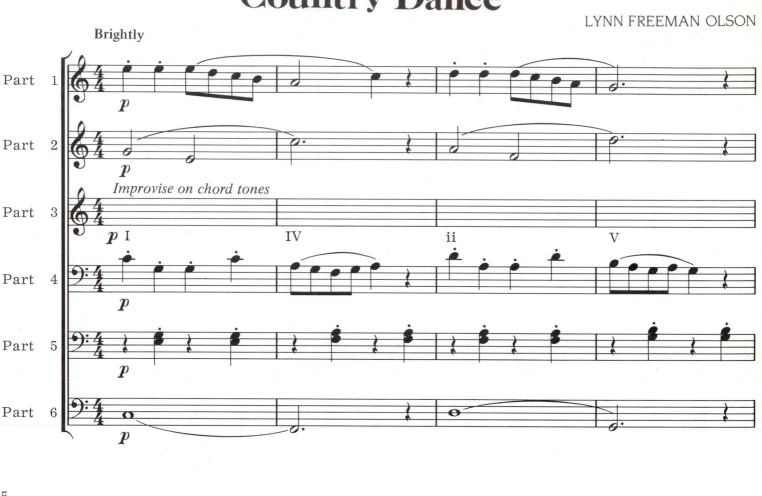

2. Play *Allegretto* by Diabelli. The Secondo part may be performed by a teacher or by a student who has had appropriate keyboard experience. (On pianos with limited range, play the lowest G's up an octave.)

Allegretto
from *Melodious Pieces*

ANTON DIABELLI, Op 149, No. 9
(1781-1858)

col 8

(8va) *   (col 8) ** - - - - - - - - - - - - - - - -

(col 8) ** -

*/** on standard range pianos

COMPOSITION

1. Complete a chordal analysis of the Persichetti *Pomp*. Use letter names for the analysis.

2. Analyze the form.

3. Does Persichetti use unique compositional techniques in *Pomp*?

4. Read through *Pomp* hands separately, blocking all chord shapes.

5. Read through *Pomp* slowly, hands together as written.

6. Compose on original piece in the style of *Pomp*.

Pomp
from *Parades for Piano*

VINCENT PERSICHETTI
(1915-   )

SUBSEQUENT REPERTOIRE

How many hand position shifts are there in *A Little Joke*?

A Little Joke
from 24 *Pieces for Children*

DMITRI KABALEVSKY, Op. 39, No. 6
(1904-   )

Notice the intervallic movement of the left hand in *Melody*.

Melody

EMIL SÖCHTING
(1858-1941)

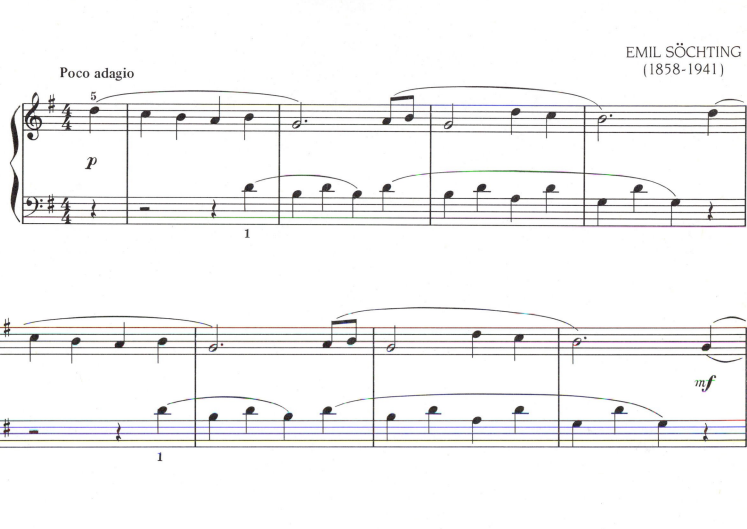

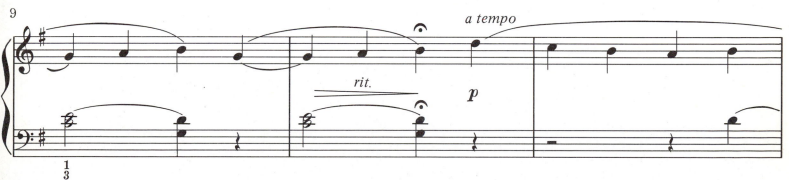

Look ahead for clef changes and shifting hand positions in *Shepherd Pipes*.

Shepherd Pipes

T. SALUTRINSKAYA

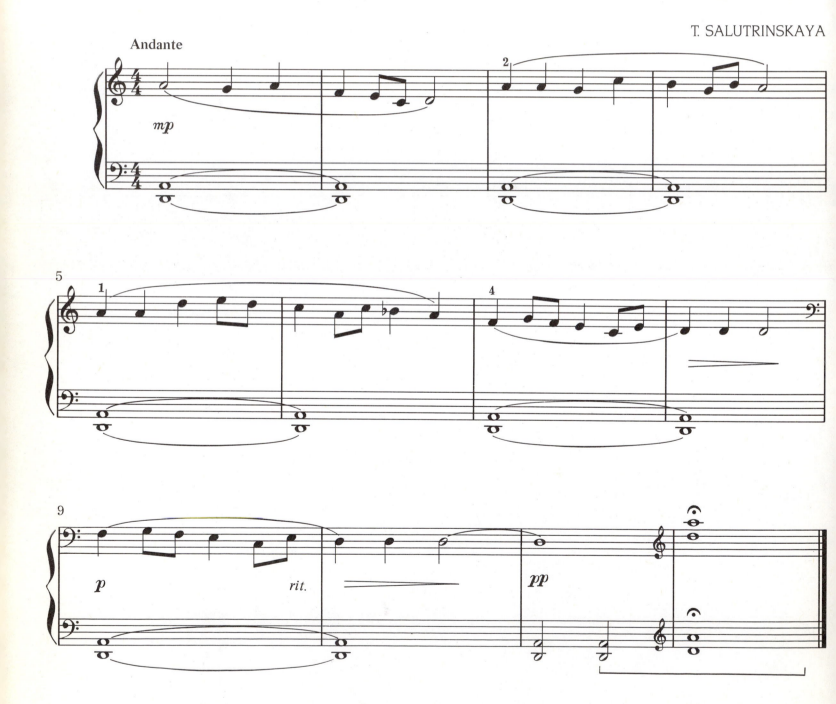

Work for an *a tempo* performance of the Persichetti *Pomp* (pages 58-59). Study dynamic and pedal markings closely.

Efficient reading includes an awareness of fragments, phrases, and sections that are repetitious. Scan *Vivace* for repetitions; then play.

Vivace

CORNELIUS GURLITT, Op. 117, No. 8
(1829-1901)

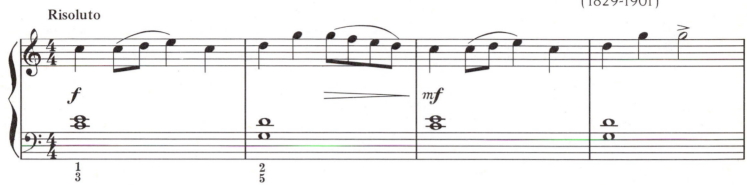

4.

Extended Use of Intervals, Pentascales and Triads / Dominant Seventh

EXEMPLARY REPERTOIRE   **Badinage**, Op. 197 Cornelius Gurlitt

INQUIRY

1. Scan the piece. Observe:

   - form
   - compostional techniques
   - range

   - phrasing
   - chromatically altered tones

2. Determine appropriate fingering, paying particular attention to middle section.

PERFORMANCE

1. Choose a partner and play *Badinage* as a duet (upper voice, Primo; lower voice, Secondo). Listen to the conversational elements as you play.

2. Play *Badinage* hands together away from the keyboard. Keep fingerings consistent.

3. Play as written with careful attention to phrasing and balance.

Badinage

CORNELIUS GURLITT, Op. 197
(1820-1901)

TOPICS TO EXPLORE AND DISCUSS

- Cornelius Gurlitt: Identify several musical contemporaries.
- Canon
- Musette: Discuss as a musical form.

RELATED SKILLS AND ACTIVITIES

TECHNIQUE

1. Play.

2. Play.

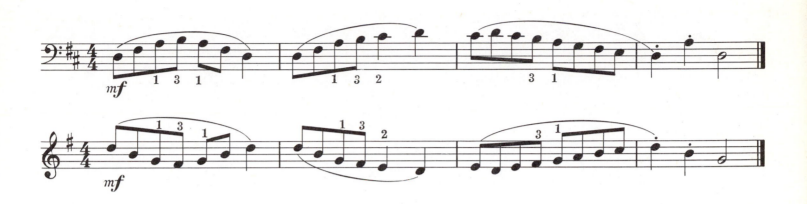

3. Play.

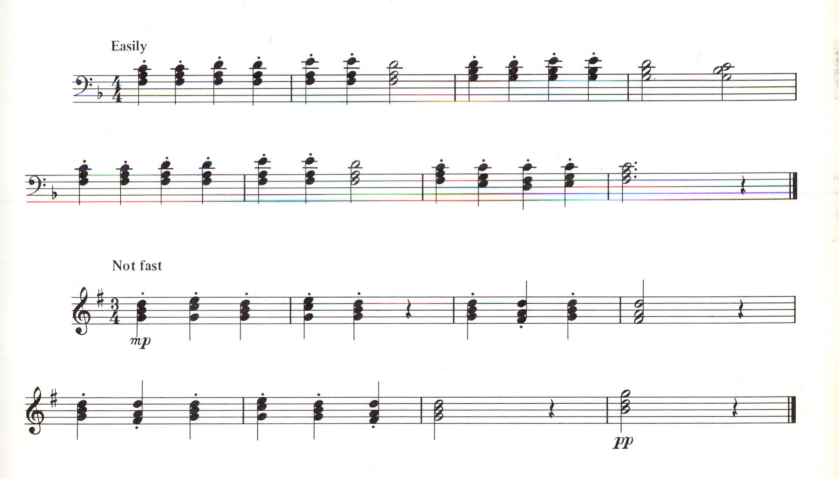

4. With one finger, play the C major pentascale and connect one tone to the next with pedal.
   The designation for pedal directs movement of the foot.

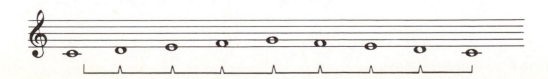

5. Play and conduct.

Andante

6. Play these progressions with the nondominant hand; conduct with the other hand.

7. Use connecting pedal and repeat item 6.

Study: Parallel and Contrary Motion

from *The First Term at the Piano*

BÉLA BARTÓK
(1881-1945)

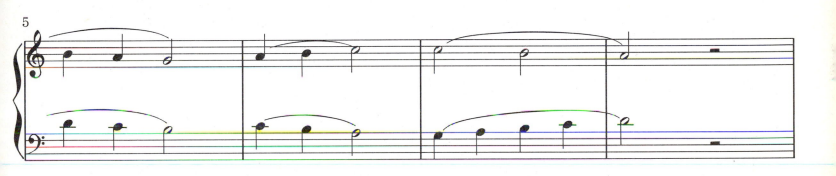

A Little Dance

from 24 *Pieces for Children*

DMITRI KABALEVSKY, Op. 39, No. 9
(1904-   )

Allegro in G

ALEXANDER REINAGLE
(1756-1809)

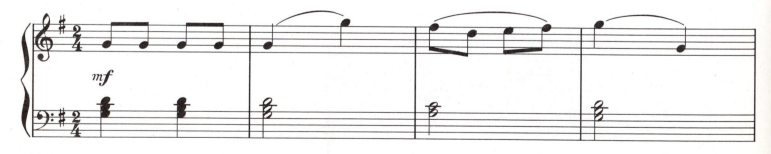

4

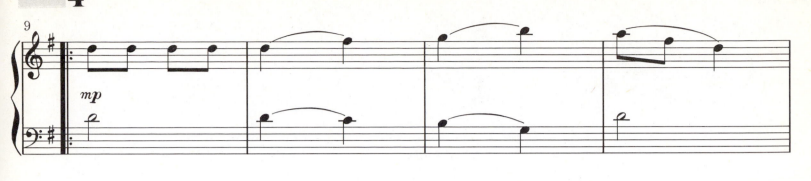

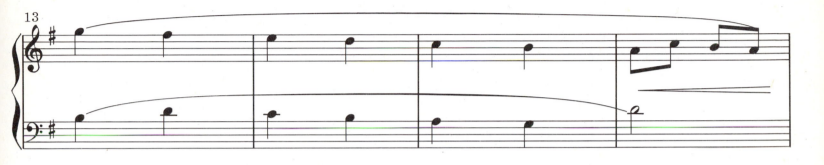

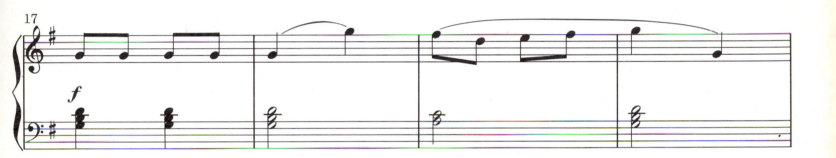

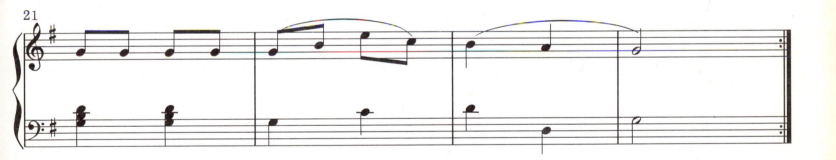

KEYBOARD THEORY

1. The root position triads in this progression move by fourths.

I   IV   I   V   I

In the left hand, double the roots of the triads and play the progression hands together.
Let the left hand also move in fourths. Play in all white-key majors.

You will have smoother motion using the *closest position* of the triads.

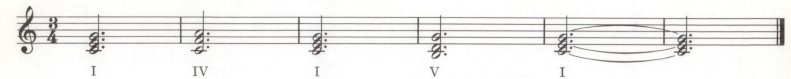

I   IV   I   V   I

To achieve the closest position, you will often move to an inversion (rearrangement) of the triad. In the preceding progression, the IV and V triads are inverted.

Using this *closest position* progression, add left-hand roots. Try both the "dominant above" and "dominant below" left-hand positions. Again, play in all white-key majors. Say the letter names of the roots as you play.

2. A dominant seventh chord (V_7) is the dominant triad plus a minor seventh above the root.

C Major
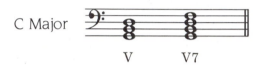

V   V7

In accompaniments, the third is often not included in the left-hand V_7 chord.

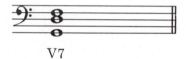

V7

For each major key shown, play a left-hand V_7 chord omitting the third. Supply the omitted third an octave higher in the right hand.

A dominant seventh naturally leads to the tonic.

V7   I

In this progression, economy of motion suggests omitting the fifth from the tonic. Play.

D major:	A major:	F major:	E major:
V7-I	V7-I	V7-I	V7-I

3. Using the following progressions, verbally spell each chord in the root position, but play the closest position.

D Major:

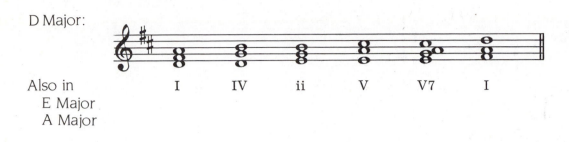

| | I | IV | ii | V | V7 | I |

Also in
  E Major
  A Major

F Major:

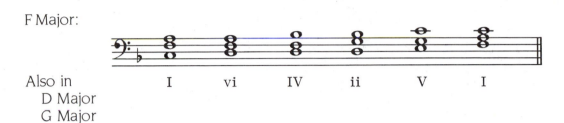

| | I | vi | IV | ii | V | I |

Also in
  D Major
  G Major

C Major:

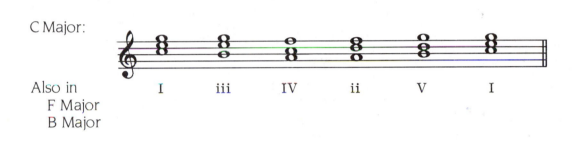

| | I | iii | IV | ii | V | I |

Also in
  F Major
  B Major

A Major:

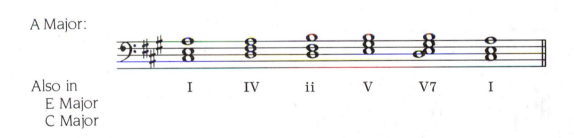

| | I | IV | ii | V | V7 | I |

Also in
  E Major
  C Major

HARMONIZATION

1. Return to the melodies on page 26, and use a two-handed accompaniment as you sing.

2. Chords may also be designated by letter name instead of Roman numeral. Harmonize the following, moving to the closest chord possible each time.

French

Left-hand melody; right-hand chords.

Easily

English

F   C7   F   C7   F

Sturdily

French

f I   V7   I   V7   I   V7   I   V7   I

3. Complete the following melodies in the style indicated.

Lively

American

mf

mf

etc.

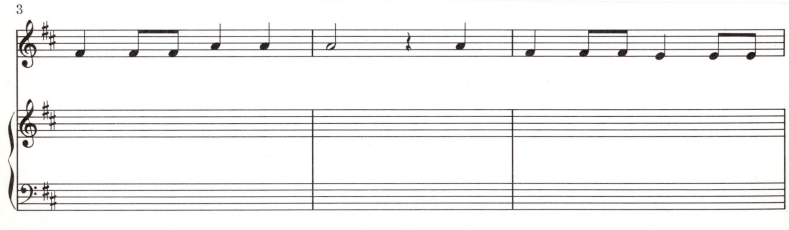

3

6

Gently

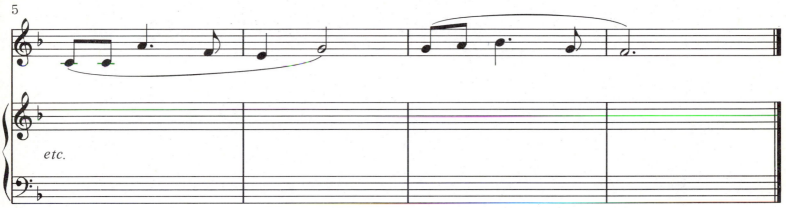

etc.

TRANSPOSITION

1. Transpose the Reinagle *Minuetto* (page 47) to A major, D major, and E major.

2. Transpose the Gurlitt *Vivace* (page 63) to F major and G major.

3. Transpose the Reinagle *Allegro in* G (page 70) to C major, D major, and E major.

4. Return to the harmonization examples on page 73-74 and transpose each to three different major keys.

IMPROVISATION

4-1

1. With left hand, play the following progression, moving to the closest chord possible (four beats per chord). With right hand, improvise a melody using chord tones only.

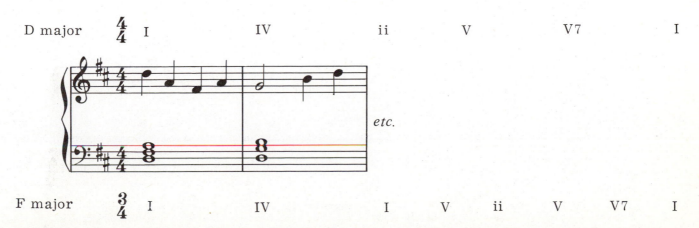

2. Rewind the Rhythm Cassette to 4-1 and play two-handed accompaniments in each key.

ENSEMBLE

Air a Bercer

from *Nous Jouons pour Maman*

ALEXANDRE TANSMAN
(1897-)

Primo

Secondo

Lullaby

LOUIS KÖHLER
(1820-1886)

Lithuanian Melody

LOUIS KÖHLER
(1820-1886)

COMPOSITION

Compose a piece using ABA form with the B section in the dominant. The composition should be a minimum of 24 measures in length.

- A section: both hands in same pentascale position (any register), using parallel and contrary motion in a two-part texture.
- B section: in the style of a musette (see Subsequent Repertoire, page 79).

SUBSEQUENT REPERTOIRE

Notice the right-hand range of *Musette* by Le Couppey. Block finger groups to provide smooth crossings. Determine a dynamic scheme.

Musette

FÉLIX LE COUPPEY
(1811-1887)

In this piece, how does the composer achieve a caressing musical quality? How does he depict the parent's underlying concern?

Lullaby

ALAN HOVHANESS
(1911-)

From: *American Composers of Today* © 1956 Marks Music Corporation. Used by permission of Hal Leonard Publishing Corporation.

Triadique

LYNN FREEMAN OLSON

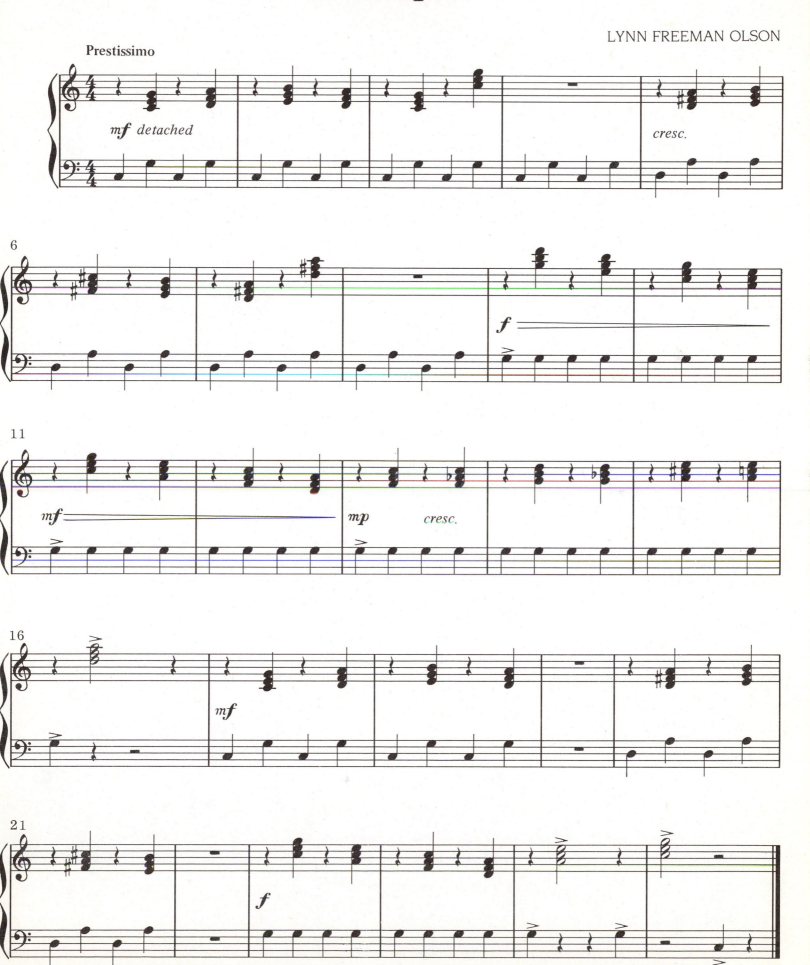

Play the right-hand chord changes in *Toreador*. Play through the left-hand melody. Then play as written.

Toreador
from *Miniatures*, Book 3

RUTH SCHONTHAL

March tempo

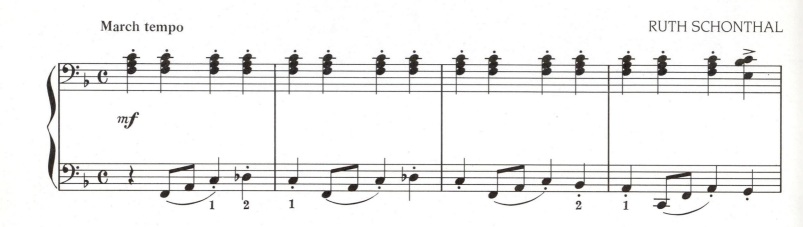

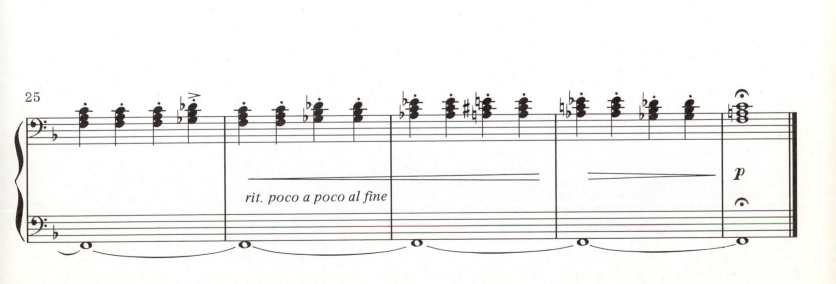

5.

Chord Shapes / Pentascales with Black - Key Groups

INQUIRY

1. Scan the piece. Observe:

- smooth motion in changing harmonies
- slur markings: actual break in sound or grouping of ideas within a longer line

PERFORMANCE

1. Play right-hand chord *changes*.

2. Establish a touch for the chords appropriate to the character of the piece.

3. Play as a duet and trade parts.

4. Use rhythmic pedaling. Once per bar is appropriate here. Why?

5. Play as written.

Modulation

from *Piano in Progress*, Vol. 1

ALEXANDRE TANSMAN
(1897-   )

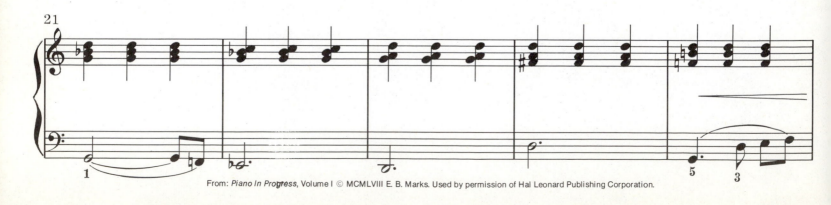

TOPICS TO EXPLORE AND DISCUSS

- Alexandre Tansman
- Modulation as related to Exemplary Repertoire, page 85.

RELATED SKILLS AND ACTIVITIES

TECHNIQUE

1. Play.

Etude

FÉLIX LE COUPPEY, Op. 17, No. 6
(1811-1887)

2. Play the following shapes.

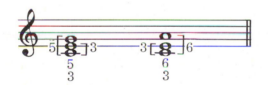

On white keys only, play a sequence of $\frac{5}{3}$ to $\frac{6}{3}$ shapes.

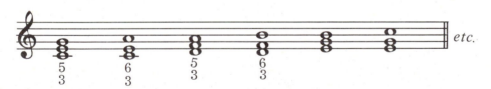

etc.

Play the same sequence with left-hand one octave lower.
Repeat the $\frac{5}{3}$ to $\frac{6}{3}$ sequence with each hand, this time sharping each F. Repeat, sharping each F and C.

3. Using a pointer finger, play and name a major pentascale on each of the following black keys.

Db/C♯   Gb/F♯

Play the two and three black-key groups hands together, blocked.

RH   2 3   2 3 4
LH   3 2   4 3 2

Play again, and this time use thumbs as pivots to move from one black-key group to the other (thumbs on F).

Using the same principle, block the pentascale. Play the pentascale again as single tones hands together.

Follow the same steps with Gb/F♯ and Cb/B (in B pentascale, left hand begins on finger 4, right hand on finger 1).

4. Play the following black-key-group pentascale drills hands separately.

5. Play the following exercises, which use chord inversions.

6. Repeat the preceding two exercises, adding connecting pedal. Let your ear be your guide.

READING

1. Focus on melodic intervals and rhythm in *Flickering Candle*.

Flickering Candle

LYNN FREEMAN OLSON

2. Play these black-key-group pieces.

3. Play the following combinations: Soprano-Baritone; Soprano-Alto-Baritone.

Morning Song

Text*

GIOVANNI PIERLUIGI DA PALESTRINA
(ca. 1525-1594)

* Aurelius Clemens Prudentius, 5th Century *Adapted by Samuel Longfellow, 1864.*

KEYBOARD THEORY

1. In a major key, the triad built on the sixth scale degree is minor.

C Major

Using the following progression, verbally spell each chord in the *root* position, but play the closest position.

C Major:

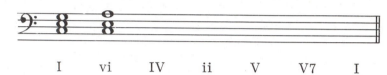

    I   vi   IV   ii   V   V7   I

Also in
   D Major
   G Major
   A Major

2. The most basic harmonic progression in music is that of dominant to tonic (V-I). In most instances, other progressions are elaborations of, and approaches to, this basic progression.

I		IV		V		I
I		IV		V	V7	I
I		IV	ii	V	V7	I
I	vi	IV	ii	V	V7	I

There is a secret life among chords. The vi has an affinity for IV—the ii is the stranger that comes in and ultimately strengthens the V-I relationship.

In V *versus* V7, there is more tension owing to the *tritone* provided by the seventh.

3. Inverted chords are nothing more than root position rearranged. Their shapes are most clearly seen through figured bass designations.

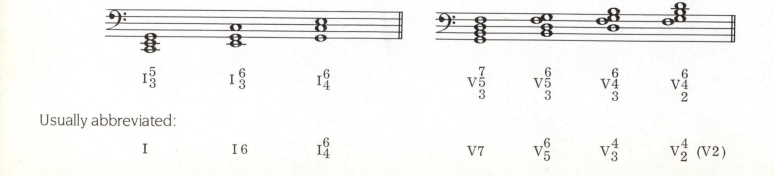

$$I_3^5 \qquad I_3^6 \qquad I_4^6 \qquad\qquad V_3^7_5 \qquad V_3^6_5 \qquad V_3^6_4 \qquad V_2^6_4$$

Usually abbreviated:

$$I \qquad\qquad I6 \qquad I_4^6 \qquad\qquad V7 \qquad V_5^6 \qquad V_3^4 \qquad V_2^4 \text{ (V2)}$$

5

All figured bass designations are built on the *lowest sounding tone,* regardless of the octave placement of the other tones.

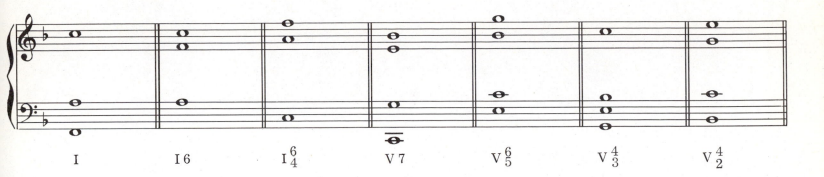

| I | I 6 | I $\frac{6}{4}$ | V 7 | V $\frac{6}{5}$ | V $\frac{4}{3}$ | V $\frac{4}{2}$ |

4. In playing four-part harmony, one may use *chorale style* or *keyboard style.*

Chorale Style   Keyboard Style

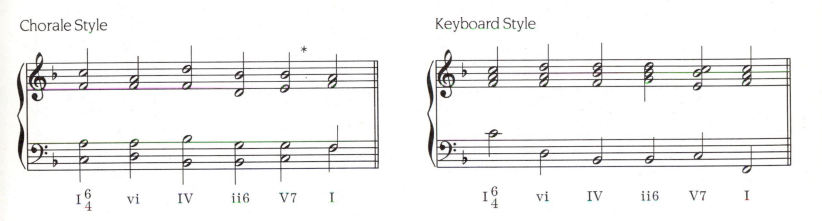

| I $\frac{6}{4}$ | vi | IV | ii6 | V7 | I | | I $\frac{6}{4}$ | vi | IV | ii6 | V7 | I |

*The tritone (E-B♭) must resolve to F-A, omitting the fifth in I.

For each following example, complete the notation of the chorale style and play. Then play in keyboard style without notating.

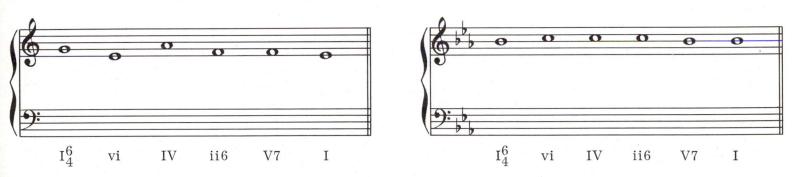

| I $\frac{6}{4}$ | vi | IV | ii6 | V7 | I | | I $\frac{6}{4}$ | vi | IV | ii6 | V7 | I |

5. Chord inversions may also be designated by letter names (guitar symbols).

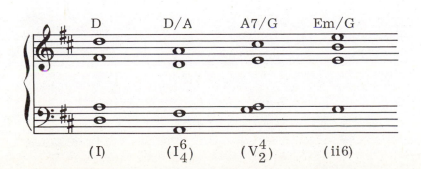

| D | D/A | A7/G | Em/G |

| (I) | (I $\frac{6}{4}$) | (V $\frac{4}{2}$) | (ii6) |

HARMONIZATION

1. The following melodies use diatonic triads and dominant sevenths. Choose several different major keys and play the melodies by ear. Then add chords. The last three melodies sound quite good done in keyboard style.

   - Try To Remember
   - Jeanie with the Light Brown Hair
   - Everybody Loves Saturday Night
   - Bingo
   - Battle Hymn of the Republic

2. Choose from I, V₇, IV, ii, vi, and iii and move to the closest possible position when harmonizing the following.

With a bounce

Traditional

f

3. Complete in the style indicated.

American

Moving quietly

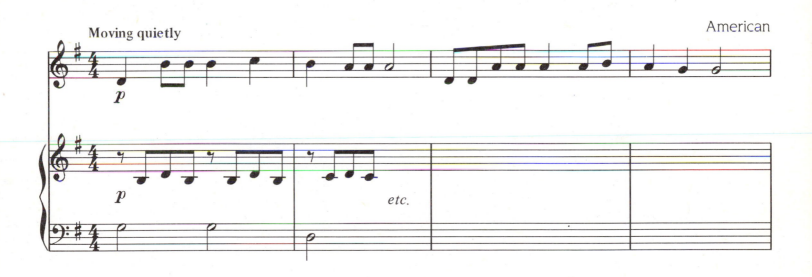

p

p   *etc.*

5

TRANSPOSITION

1. Transpose the following to D major and F major.

Moderately

MARTHA HILLEY

2. Transpose the Verdi example to A major and F major *before* playing in the written key. Observe inversions.

GIUSEPPE VERDI
(1833-1901)

Andante

IMPROVISATION

5-1

1. Improvise a melody using chord tones only. The Rhythm Cassette will set the tempo.

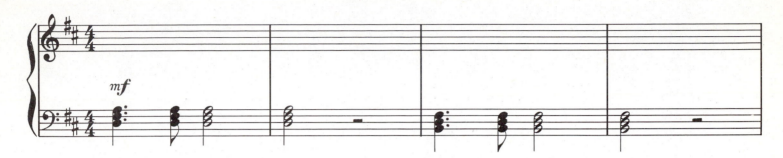

2. The following melodies may be played using black keys only.

- Old MacDonald
- Merrily We Roll Along
- Amazing Grace
- Auld Lang Syne

Play through each and improvise an ostinato bass.

5-2

3. Using the following progression, play right-hand chords, moving to the closest chord possible.

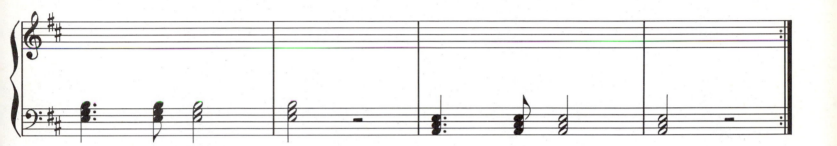

E Major: $\frac{4}{4}$ I | vi | IV | ii | V | I ii6 | I$_4^6$ V7 | I ‖

D Major: $\frac{3}{4}$

F Major: $\frac{6}{8}$

B Major: $\frac{5}{8}$

Rewind the Rhythm Cassette to 5-2 and repeat the progressions, this time adding the roots of chords in left hand except where inversion is indicated.

Rewind again and repeat the progressions, using left-hand chord roots while improvising right-hand melodies based on chord tones.

ENSEMBLE

5-3

Jingle, Jangle, Jingle
(I Got Spurs)

JOSEPH J. LILLEY
Arranged by Lynn Freeman Olson

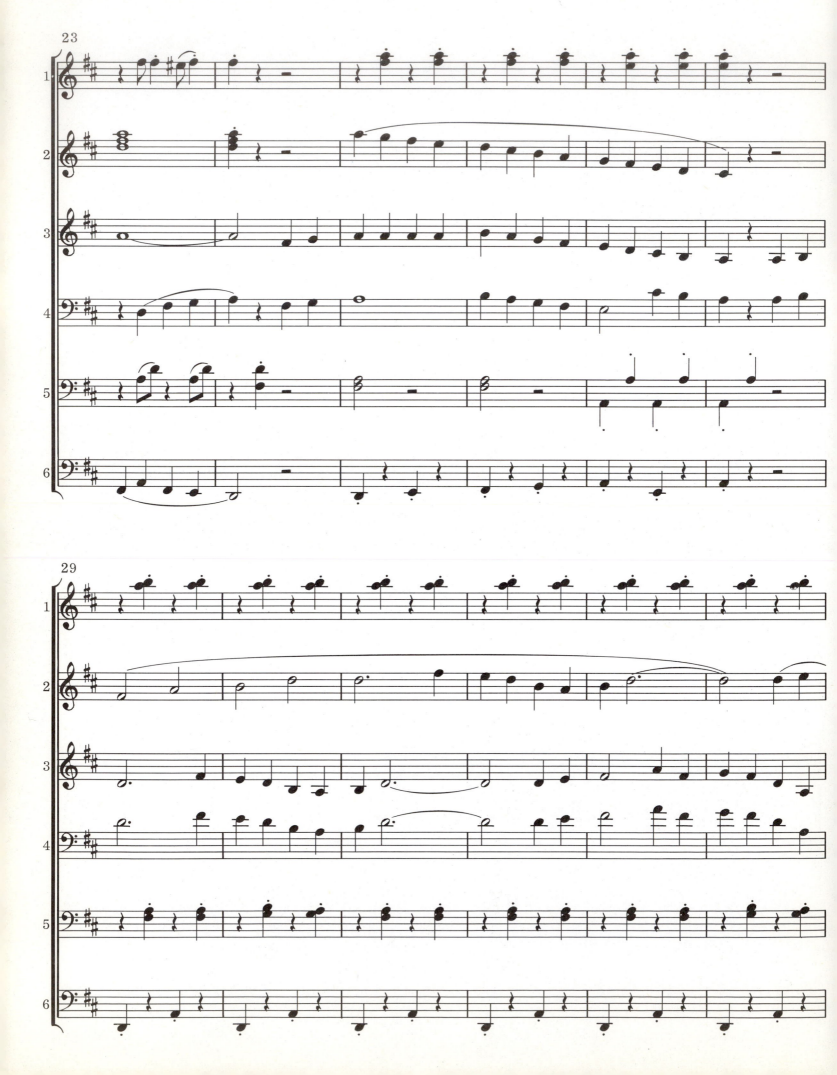

Vanya

from *50 Russian Folk Songs*

PETER ILYICH TCHAIKOVSKY
(1840-1893)

COMPOSITION

With a partner, create an ABA duet. Secondo plays two-handed broken chord accompaniment; Primo plays one-handed melody based on chord tones. For the B section, Primo and Secondo switch parts.

Use the following harmonic progression in the key and meter of your choice.

I   vi   IV   ii   V   I   ii6   I$^6_4$ V7   I

The same harmonic scheme may be used for the A and B sections.

SUBSEQUENT REPERTOIRE

Compare contour in measures 1-4, 5-8. Label harmony in measures 9-16.

Etude

JEAN-BAPTISTE DUVERNOY, Op. 176, No. 24
(1800-1880)

Determine fingering.

Rigaudon

ALEXANDER GOEDICKE
(1877-1957)

Name and play the chord shapes used by Purcell.

Preludio

HENRY PURCELL
(1659-1695)

Do a harmonic analysis before playing the Beethoven. Include indications of inversions.

German Dance

LUDWIG van BEETHOVEN, WoO 42
(1770-1827)

Musical Evaluation Chapter

All inquiry and direction in *Piano for the Developing Musician* are designed to promote self-teaching. To help you evaluate your progress toward this goal, we have eliminated inquiry and performance directions from the materials on pages 108-117. Supply the missing verbiage and complete the activities.

EXEMPLARY REPERTOIRE   **Risoluto** Bach/Ricci

INQUIRY

1.

PERFORMANCE

1.

Risoluto

JOHANN CHRISTIAN BACH/
FRANCESCO PASQUALE RICCI ''METHOD''

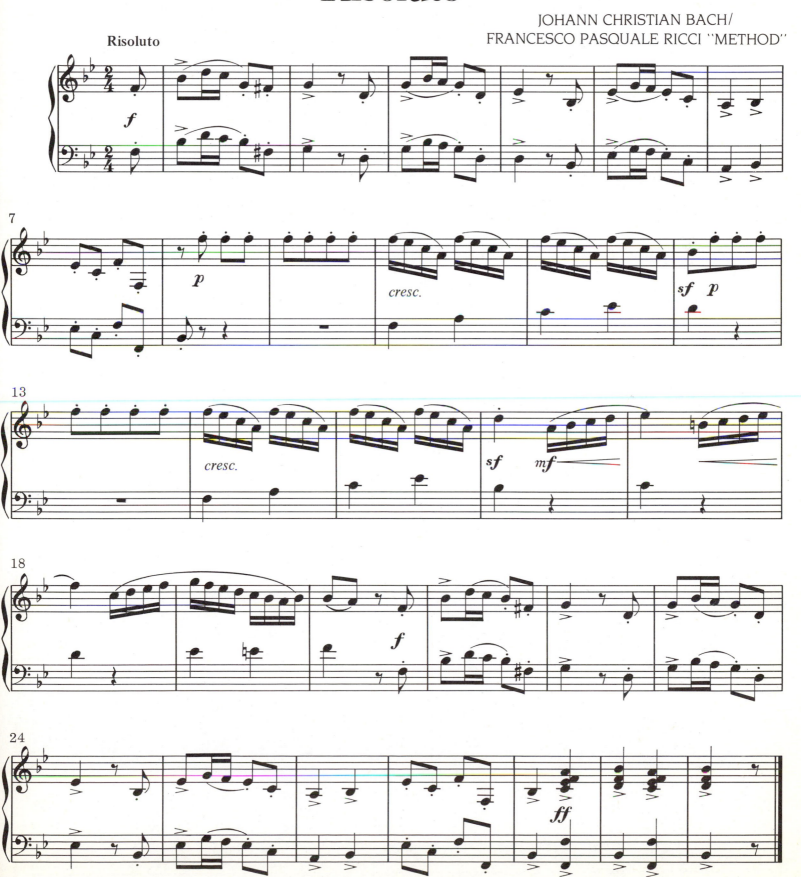

TOPICS TO EXPLORE AND DISCUSS

- •
- •

RELATED SKILLS AND ACTIVITIES

TECHNIQUE

1.

2.

3.

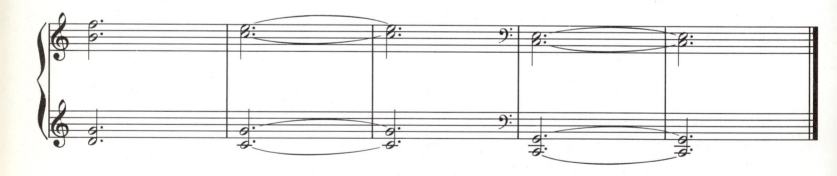

4.

5.

Benediction

JOSEPH M. MARTIN

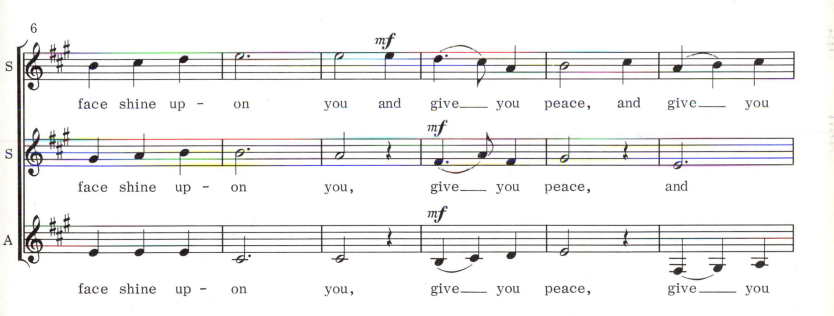

KEYBOARD THEORY

1.

    I   IV   V   I   vi   iii   IV   ii   V   I

2.

HARMONIZATION

American

MEC

TRANSPOSITION

1.

2.

Soldier's Song

LOUIS KÖHLER
(1820-1886)

IMPROVISATION

1. $\frac{2}{4}$ I | I | vi | vi | IV | IV | I16 | V7 | I ‖

2.

ENSEMBLE

Under the Bamboo Tree

COLE & JOHNSON
Arranged by Lynn Freeman Olson

MEC

name;— 'Cause I love-a you and love-a you true, And if you- a love-a me,

simile

One live as two, two live as one, Un-der the bam-boo tree.

Spoken: Wow Wow Wow

SUBSEQUENT REPERTOIRE

Before playing the Gurlitt, ...

Der kleine Schelm

CORNELIUS GURLITT, Op. 117, No. 18
(1820-1901)

Based on the preceding pages of evaluation and your perception of personal growth in musicianship at the keyboard, briefly describe your current status relevant to the scope and sequence of PDM. Include in your thinking:

- Analytical incisiveness

- Musical performance, solo and ensemble

- Technique

- Reading

- Keyboard theory

- Harmonization

- Transposition

- Improvisation

- Composition

6.

Scalar Sequences/Modal Patterns/ Black-Key-Group Major Scales

EXEMPLARY REPERTOIRE   **Prelude,** Op. 37, No. 5 Giuseppe Concone

INQUIRY

    1. Scan the piece. Observe:

        • scalar sequences
        • clef changes
        • open chord structure: root position and inversion (analysis)
        • chromatic scale

PERFORMANCE

    1. Play the following sequence on a flat surface.

    2. Play the following sequence on a flat surface.

    Repeat several times until postition shift is secure.

3. Play the first four measures from the score, repeating the right-hand scalar pattern.

4. A common fingering for the chromatic scale is:

   white to black—1 to 3
   white to white—1 to 2

   Play the three-octave chromatic scale from the score.

5. Play all bass tones and chords in rhythm. (Teacher fills in scalar passages.)

6. Look away from the score and "talk it through."

7. Take a deep breath and play as written.

Prelude

GIUSSEPPE CONCONE, Op 37, No. 5
(1801-1861)

TOPICS TO EXPLORE AND DISCUSS

- Giuseppe Concone
- Stylistic parallels between Concone and Chopin
- Samuil Maykapar

RELATED SKILLS AND ACTIVITIES

TECHNIQUE

1. Chromatic exercises:

- Using the principles of chromatic scale fingering stated on page 120, determine a right-hand fingering for the following example.

- Play with right hand.
- Determine a left-hand fingering for the same example and play left hand one octave lower.
- Play hands together, paying particular attention to fingerings for natural half steps.

2. Play the following as written with the nondominant hand.

Play again. This time fill in the rests by playing C's (when you end a pattern on C) or G's (when you end on G) with the other hand.

Swing the exercise by playing the eighths in a long-short pattern ♩♪ and syncopating the fill-in tones.

3. In Chapter 5 you used the black-key-group fingering principle. This principle forms the basis of fingering for the following major scales.

D♭/C♯   G♭/F♯   C♭/B

- Block the D♭ major scale hands together, two octaves up and down.

2 blacks—thumbs—3 blacks—thumbs, etc.

6-1

- Play the D♭ major scale as individual tones. Keep fingers close to the keys, covering positions as shifts occur. Use the directions and background provided by the Rhythm Cassette.

- Transfer the same principle to the other black-key-group scales and play using the Rhythm Cassette.

READING

1. Play the following.

Die Tonleiter

DANIEL GOTTLOB TÜRK
(1756-1813)

* Original key, D Major

6

2. Play the following.

Tag

from *Piano Music for Children*, Vol. 1

SOULIMA STRAVINSKY
(1910-   )

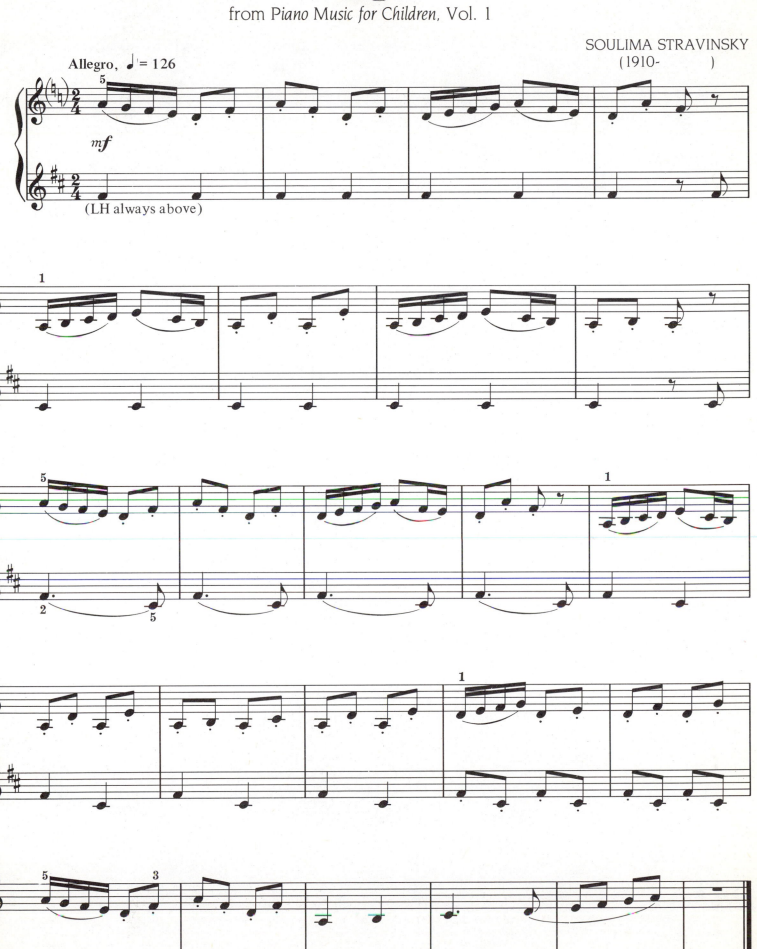

3. Play as written.

Allegro

STREABBOG (JEAN-LOUIS GOBBAERTS),Op. 63, No. 2
(1835-1886)

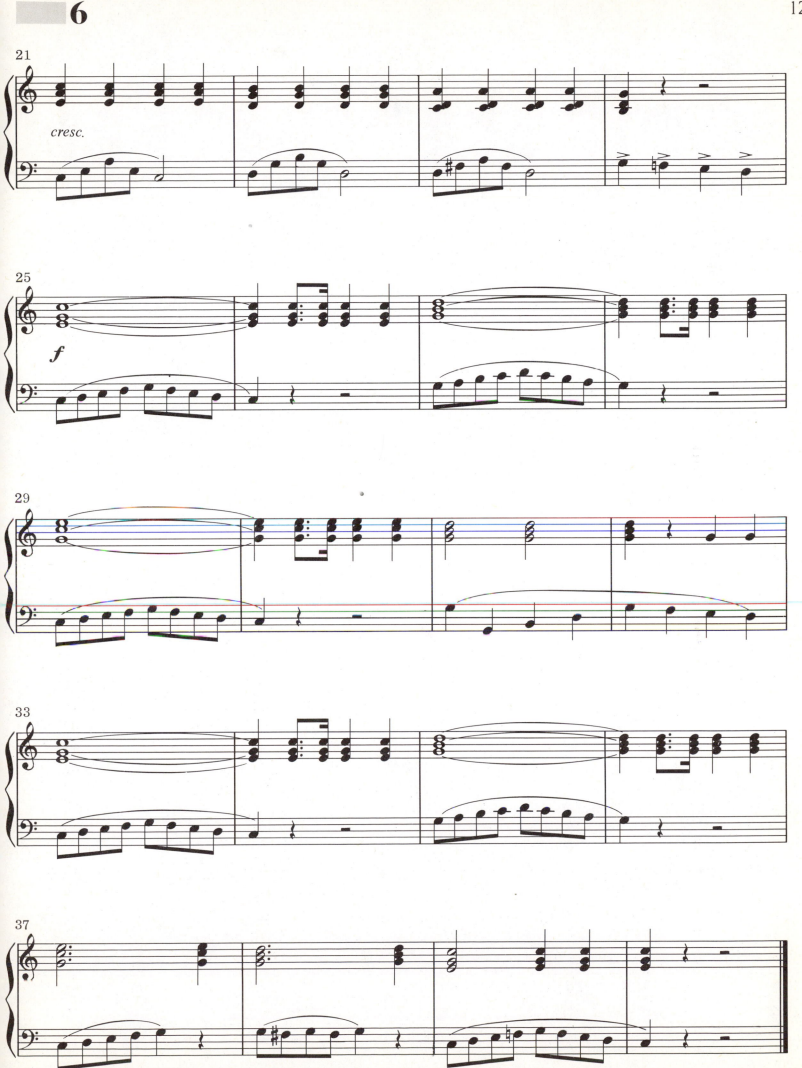

KEYBOARD THEORY

1. Think the key of D♭ major and play a scale beginning on the second degree and ending on the second degree an octave higher. This is the E♭ *Dorian* mode. We can build seven different modes starting on the seven tones of a major scale.

- Ionian—1st degree (major scale)
- Dorian—2nd degree
- Phrygian—3rd degree
- Lydian—4th degree
- Mixolydian—5th degree
- Aeolian—6th degree (natural minor)
- Locrian—7th degree

Think the B major key signature and play a scale beginning on the second scale degree and ending on C♯ an octave above. This is the C♯ Dorian mode.

Experiment with other modal scales. Always think of the major key signature. (Suggestions: C♯ Ionian; C Locrian; A♭ Dorian).

HARMONIZATION

FRANZ SCHUBERT
(1797-1828)

DANIEL D. EMMETT
(1815-1904)

Moderately

Traditional

Lively

I ii$\frac{6}{4}$ V6 I

vi ii6 V7 I

Shaker

Moderately

6

HENRI A. CESAR MALAN
(1787-1804)

JEAN SIBELIUS
(1865-1957)

6

Shaker

'Tis the gift to be sim - ple, 'tis the gift to be free; 'Tis the

gift to come down where we ought to be; And when we find our-selves in the

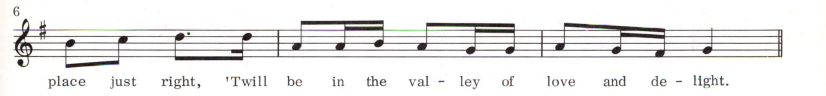

place just right, 'Twill be in the val - ley of love and de - light.

When true sim - plic - i - ty is gained, To bow and to bend we

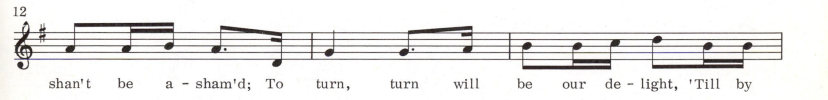

shan't be a - sham'd; To turn, turn will be our de - light, 'Till by

turn - ing, turn - ing we come round right.

130

6
American

TRANSPOSITION

    1. Transpose the Czerny to C♯, F♯ and B major; C Dorian.

Dance

CARL CZERNY, Op. 823, No. 11
(1791-1857)

    2. Transpose the Türk *Die Tonleiter* (page 122) to G♭ major and G Dorian. Determine a logical fingering for G Dorian.

3. Transpose *The Chase* to E and A major.

The Chase
from *First Lessons for the Piano*

CORNELIUS GURLITT, Op. 117, No. 15
(1820-1901)

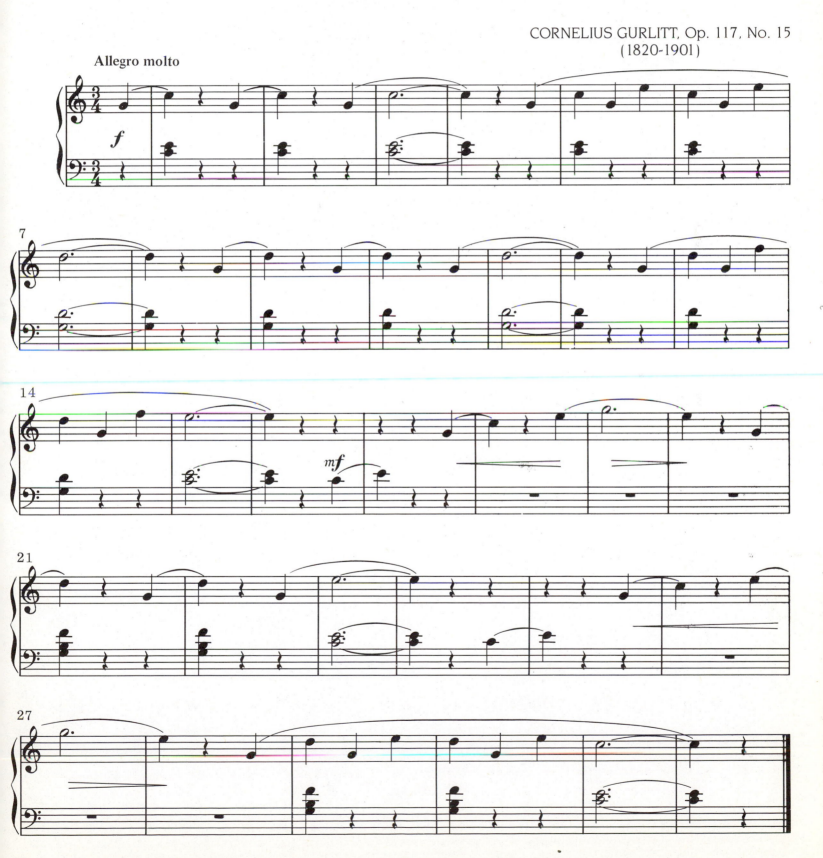

4. Transpose *Plaint* so that

- tonic is G
- tonic is D

What is the signature for each new key?

Plaint

LYNN FREEMAN OLSON

Adagietto

IMPROVISATION

1. Using the A♭ Mixolydian scale, improvise a right-hand melody above the following left-hand chord progression.

I   IV   I   I   V   V   I   I

6-2

Play along with the Rhythm Cassette.

2. Using the following progression

4/4 I | vi | IV | ii | V | I ii6 | I$^6_4$ V7 | I ‖

play:

- left-hand chords; closest possible position
- right-hand chords; closest possible position

3. Rewind the Rhythm Cassette to 6-1 and play both activities straight through without stopping. Try several different keys.

ENSEMBLE

Shuffle

SUSAN OGILVY

Parts 2 and 3 of the Satie are to be played by one pianist.

Gnossienne No. 2

ERIK SATIE
(1866-1925)
Arranged by Lynn Freeman Olson

Later, all three parts may be played by one pianist.

COMPOSITION

Create modal pieces to match the words of these two poems by Ogden Nash.

1. For "The Panther," use C Dorian.

The Panther

The panther is like a leopard,
Except it hasn't been peppered.
Should you behold a panther crouch,
Prepare to say Ouch.
Better yet, if called by a panther,
Don't anther.

2. For "The Pizza," use G Lydian.

The Pizza

Look at itsy-bitsy Mitzi!
See her figure slim and ritzy!
She eatsa
Pizza!
Greedy Mitzi!
She no longer itsy-bitsy!

SUBSEQUENT REPERTOIRE

On what scale is the Bartók based?

Peasant's Song
from *Ten Easy Pieces*

BÉLA BARTÓK
(1881-1945)

Play the left-hand changes of the Concone Etude. Play as written.

Etude

GIUSEPPE CONCONE, Op. 24, No. 8
(1801-1861)

Andantino un poco mosso

6

Name and play the mode on which the Stevens work is based.

An Ancient Roundelay

from *Modal Miniatures*

EVERETT STEVENS

* All appoggiaturas to be struck simultaneously with chord, then released immediately

From: *Modal Miniatures* © 1957 Oliver Ditson Company. Used by permission of the publisher.

** Play loco on pianos of limited range

Plan for the articulation changes in *Autumn*.

Autumn

SAMUIL MAYKAPAR, Op. 28
(1867-1938)

6

 145

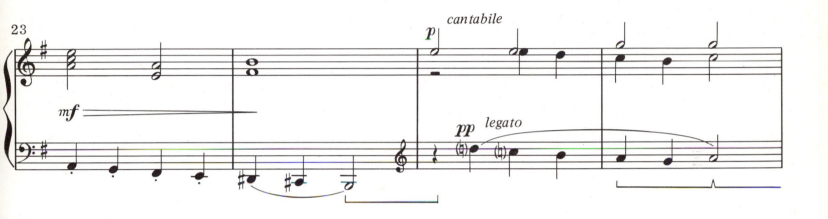

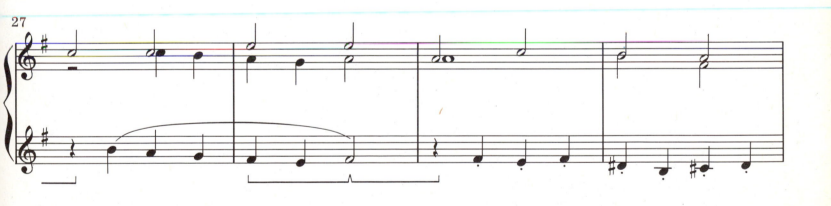

7.

White-Key Major Scale Fingerings / Blues Pentascale and the 12-Bar Blues

INQUIRY

1. Scan the piece. Observe:

   - melodic sequence
   - harmonic sequence—modulation to dominant
   - form
   - beaming of eighth notes

     French (and some Italian) Baroque performance practices suggest slight unevenness (♩³♪) to duple eighths beamed in pairs (*notes inégales*) and even sounds when more than two eighths are beamed together. This practice is inappropriate in fast tempi. What is the effect of *notes inégales*? Are there any modern counterparts to this technique?

2. Determine logical fingering with particular attention to melodic cadences and smooth left-hand movement.

3. Decide dynamic levels to enhance form.

PERFORMANCE

1. Rehearse left hand.

2. Perform right hand in the appropriate style.

3. Perform hands together.

Menuet en Rondeau

JEAN-PHILLIPE RAMEAU
(1683-1764)

Allegretto

TOPICS TO EXPLORE AND DISCUSS

- Jean-Phillipe Rameau and his contemporaries
- *Traité de L'Harmonie,* 1722
- Origin of the blues
- Scat syllables

RELATED SKILLS AND ACTIVITIES

TECHNIQUE

1. The following is traditional C major scale fingering (two octaves).

RH	1	2	⬭3	1	2	⬭3	4	☐1	2	⬭3	1	2	⬭3	4	5
LH	5	4	3	2	1	3	2	1	4	3	2	1	3	2	1

7-1

Away from the keyboard on a flat surface, play the scale upward and downward. Say "3's" and "1's" when those fingers play together. Now play on the keyboard, slowly and steadily. This fingering is also used for D major, E major, G major, and A major. Play scales as directed by the Rhythm Cassette.

2. Play the C major scale upward and stop on A. Now *flat* the A and continue with the same finger combinations to play the scale of A♭ major.

3. Rewind Rhythm Cassette to 6-1 and review black-key scales as directed on page 122.

READING

1. On what scale is the Bartók *Song* based?

Song

from *For Children*, Vol. 1

BÉLA BARTÓK
(1881-1945)

2. Determine fingering.

Common Tones
from *Happy Time*

ALEXANDRE TANSMAN
(1897-   )

Moderato

3. Plan right-hand scale crossings.

Allemande

LUDWIG van BEETHOVEN
(1770-1827)

4. Describe elements of unity in the Mozart.

Minuet

WOLFGANG AMADEUS MOZART, K. 6
(1756-1791)

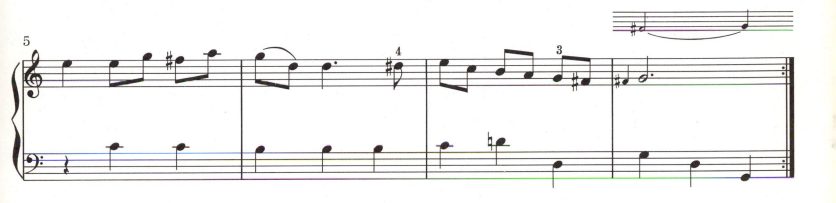

KEYBOARD THEORY

1. The note given is the leading tone in a major key. Play a *keyboard style* cadence pattern, V₇-I, with the leading tone and its neighbor tonic in the soprano voice.

Example:

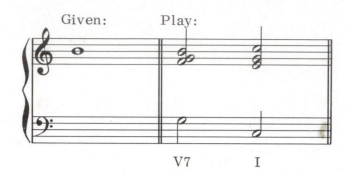

2. In which major scales can the following melodic intervals function as written?

Play each scale and sing only the given interval in numerals.

3. The numerals here refer to scale degrees. Complete a major scale upward on the keyboard while singing the degree numbers. Finish with a tonic root position triad.

Example:

4. Play the following in three major keys using right hand only.

5. For each example, give the key signature and then play the modal scale (decide fingering).

- Phrygian on F
- Locrian on G
- Lydian on D♭

- Dorian on B
- Mixolydian on F♯
- Aeolian on E

HARMONIZATION

A Round

JOHN HILTON
(1599-1657)

Complete the following harmonization in the style indicated.

American

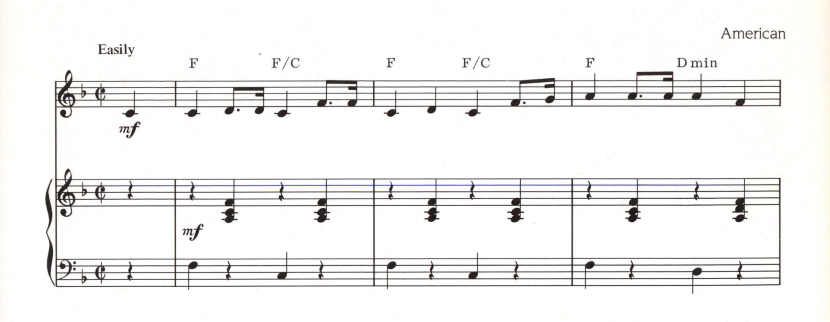

etc.

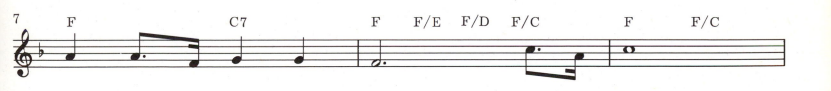

TRANSPOSITION

1. Transpose the Concone *Prelude in* B-*flat* (page 120) to C major. Plan a fingering that will facilitate transposing the same prelude to B major.

2. Play the following exercises in the transposed keys first as you conduct.

Transpose to A♭ and E♭ major.

Transpose to F♯ and B major.

Transpose to B♭ and E major.

Andante

Transpose to A and C♯ major.

3. Transpose the following examples to A, E, and A♭ majors. Use traditional scale fingerings.

Moderato

Moderato

Moderato

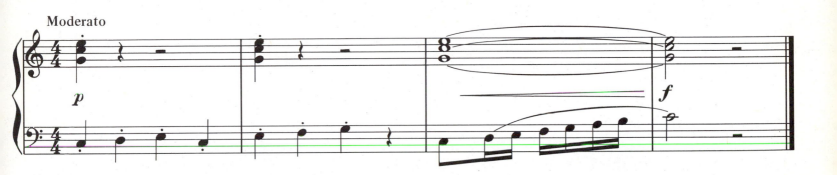

IMPROVISATION

1. The blues pentascale is 1, 4, and 5 of a major pentascale with a flat 3 and an added flat 5.

Key of C: C, E♭, F, G♭, G♮

In beginning blues improvisation, this pentascale provides a foolproof vehicle because the melodic tones fit the basic harmonies used.

Play:

I   IV   V   I

7-2

Traditional blues eighths are played with a swing, much the same as *notes inégales*, but with the emphasis on the second note in each pair. Play the preceding example as the Rhythm Cassette emphasizes blues eighths.

7-3

2. *Scat syllables* offer a natural model for rhythmic ideas in blues improvisation. Practice the following syllables with the Rhythm Cassette. Directions are narrated.

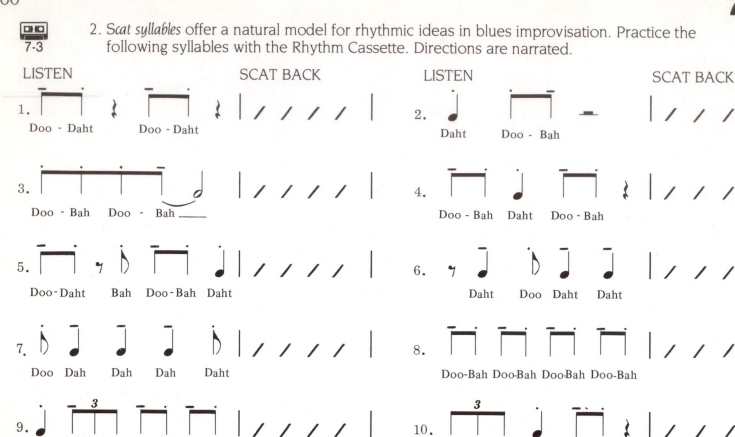

7-4

3. The following 12 bars of scat show a possibility for melodic rhythm in one chorus of blues. Scat along with the Rhythm Cassette.

Rewind the Rhythm Cassette to 7-4. Scat the 12 bars again and play the syllables you are using within the G blues pentascale.

Rewind the Rhythm Cassette again to 7-4 and repeat the pentascale scats, this time adding left-hand open fifths. Follow this blues progression.

I	IV	I	I
IV	IV	I	I
V	IV	I	I

7
ENSEMBLE

Piccola fuga á due

TITO MATTEI
(1841-1914)

Perform *Blue Sound* using the Rhythm Cassette background.

All ♩♩ are played rounded to ♩³♪

Blue Sound

LYNN FREEMAN OLSON

Moving

Part
3

Moving

Part
4

detached

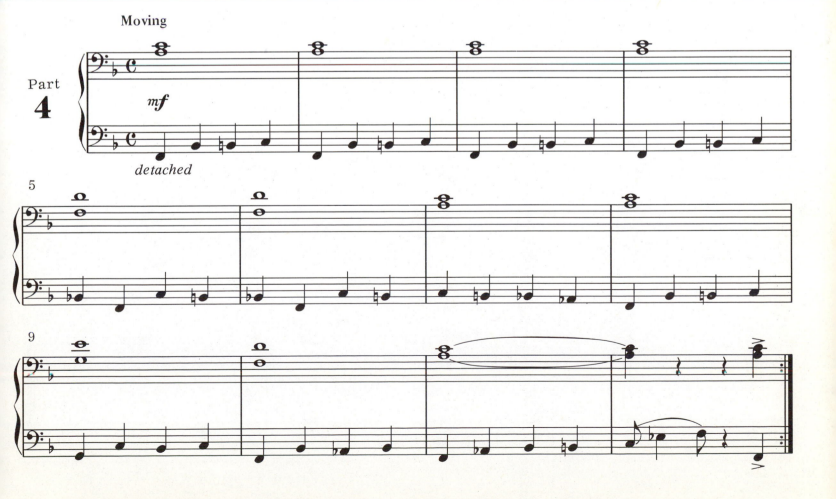

COMPOSITION

Play through *Dripping Faucet* by Alan Shulman. Compose a light "descriptive miniature."

Dripping Faucet

ALAN SHULMAN
(1915-)

SUBSEQUENT REPERTOIRE

Plan the clef changes in the Biggs.

On the Perfect 5th

from *Twelve Little Etudes*

JOHN BIGGS

Twelve Little Etudes available from CONSORT PRESS, 1717 North State College, Fullerton, CA 92631

Locate all examples of broken chords, sequential patterns, scale passages, and repetition in this sonatina movement.

Sonatina

from *Analytical Sonatinas*

FRANK LYNES, Op. 39, No. 1
(1858-1913)

Compare the couplets with the theme.

Play Theme, Couplet 1, Theme, Couplet 2, and Theme.

Tambourin

LOUIS-CLAUDE DAQUIN
(1694-1772)

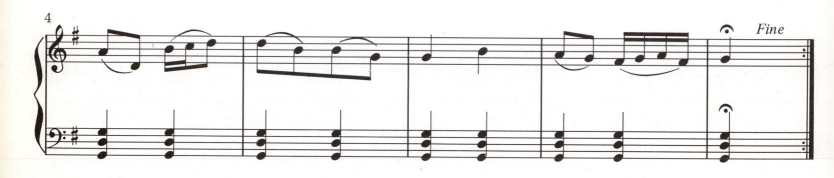

COUPLET 2

D.C. al Fine

Study the first four bars and determine the mode; compare the next four bars. Complete the analysis.

Harvest Dance

JOHN CHAGY

8.

White-Key Minor Scale Fingerings
Diatonic Harmonies in Minor

Homage to Bartók Pál Kadosa

INQUIRY

Scan the piece. Observe:

• quality of each triad

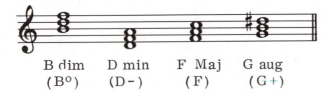

B dim   D min   F Maj   G aug
(B°)   (D−)   (F)   (G+)

In root position:

a diminished triad consists of a minor third and a diminished fifth.
a minor triad consists of a minor third and a perfect fifth.
a major triad consists of a major third and a perfect fifth.
an augmented triad consists of a major third and an augmented fifth.

• length of the first rhythmic phrase. What are the lengths of the subsequent rhythmic phrases?
• dynamic organization
• patterns of contrary motion

PERFORMANCE

1. On a flat surface, tap the rhythm of the entire piece, observing dynamics and direction of hand movement.

2. Play as written.

Homage to Bartók

PÁL KADOSA
(1903-   )

TOPICS TO EXPLORE AND DISCUSS

- Parallel *versus* relative minor
- Natural, harmonic, melodic minors
- Pál Kadosa

RELATED SKILLS AND ACTIVITIES

TECHNIQUE

1. Determine fingering for each and play.

Transpose to D Phrygian, B Lydian, and D Mixolydian.

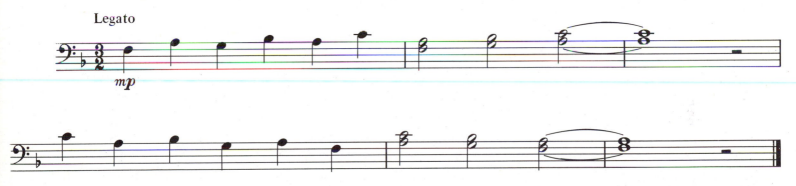

Transpose to four other major keys.

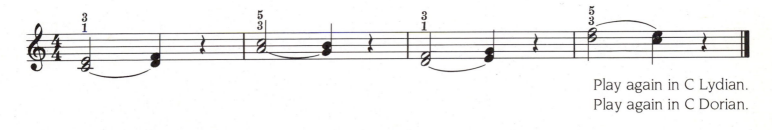

Play again in C Lydian.
Play again in C Dorian.

Play again in C Mixolydian.
Play again in C Aeolian.

2. Rewind the Rhythm Cassette to 7-1 and review the major scales from page 149.

READING

    1. Play *Melody*. Plan pedaling based on harmony.

Melody

DENNIS RILEY

8

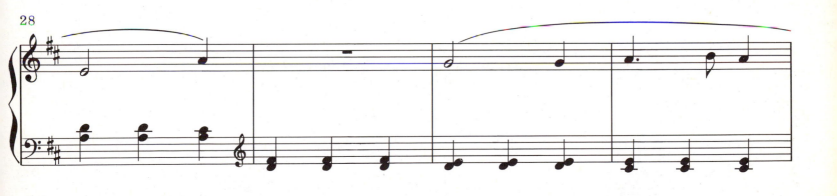

2. Play *Sadness* after analyzing the harmonic implications.

Sadness

DANIEL GOTTLOB TÜRK
(1756-1813)

3. vocal tenor clef. Actual sound is an octave lower than written.

Das Morgenrot

ROBERT PRACHT

4. Play the Czerny with attention to articulation.

Folk Melody

CARL CZERNY
(1791-1857)

5. Play the *Austrian Waltz* after identifying sequences.

Austrian Waltz

CARL CZERNY
(1791-1857)

1. Play triads on each tone of the major scale as indicated.

Root on top:

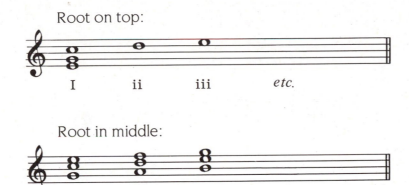

I   ii   iii   *etc.*

Root in middle:

I   ii   iii   *etc.*

2. Play this triad sequence with root on top. Play in all major keys except B♭ and E♭.

I → iii   ii → IV   iii → V   IV → vi   V → vii°   vi → I   vii° → ii → I

Play again, doubling the root in the bass.

Play the same triad sequence with the root in middle. Repeat with left-hand doubled root.

3. All minor scales are derived from their relative majors and use the same key signatures. The natural minor scale can be observed within the major scale pattern, beginning on the sixth scale degree.

There are two commonly used altered forms of the natural minor scale. The *harmonic* form is the result of the major quality of the dominant seventh chord and therefore uses an accidental to produce a leading tone that is a half step below tonic.

The *melodic* form uses an additional accidental in the ascending pattern to avoid the awkward augmented second.

When descending, melodic returns to the natural form of the minor.

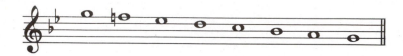

4. The following white-key minor scales use the same fingering as their parallel major scales. Refer to the fingerings used on page 149.

   • C natural, harmonic, and melodic minor
   • D natural, harmonic, and melodic minor
   • E natural, harmonic, and melodic minor
   • G natural, harmonic, and melodic minor
   • A natural, harmonic, and melodic minor

Play these minor scales as directed by the Rhythm Cassette.

5. *Diatonic triads in minor.* Play the following triads in D minor.

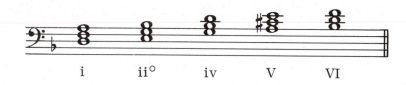

Using the following progression, verbally spell each chord in root position, but play the closest position.

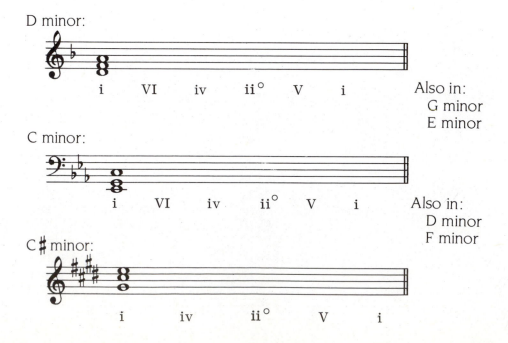

HARMONIZATION

1. Add a bass line to Stephen Foster's *Camptown Races* on page 155.

2. Harmonize the following with chords given. When an inversion is indicated, that position must be used; when none is indicated, use the principle of closest possible position.

Spanish

3. Complete the following.

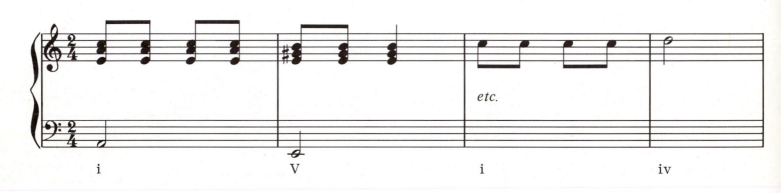

Russian

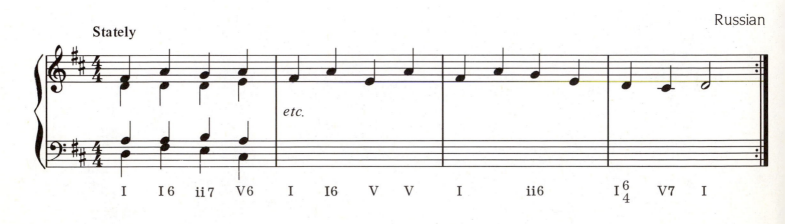

4. Play the following melodies by ear and determine appropriate harmonies for each.

- *Greensleeves*
- *Joshua Fit the Battle*
- *Motherless Child*

8-2

5. Play several types of two-handed accompaniments based on the following progressions. The Rhythm Cassette will determine tempo.

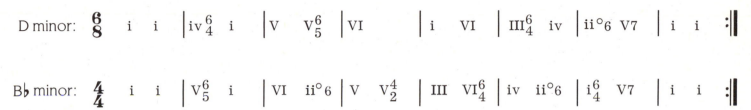

TRANSPOSITION

1. Transpose the *Tambourin* by Daquin (page 168) to D major and A major.

2. Transpose *Hopak* by Goedicke to the natural and harmonic forms of G minor.

Hopak

ALEXANDER GOEDICKE
(1877-1957)

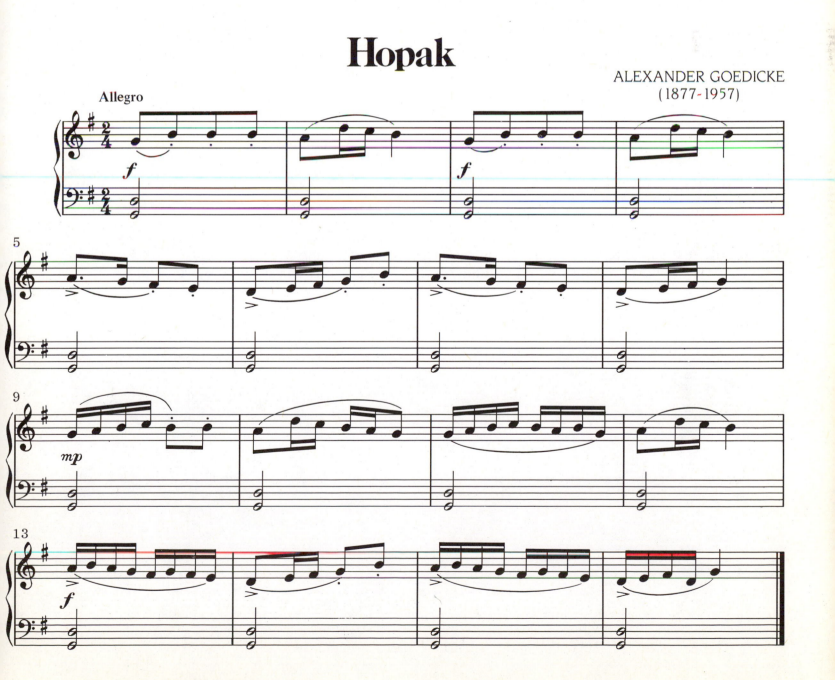

IMPROVISATION

1. Play the following expansion of the blues pentascale in F.

Rewind the Rhythm Cassette to 7-4 and use the expanded blues pentascale in G major. Use scat syllables.

2. The beginning 12-bar blues progression is based on three chords, I, IV, V. To expand this harmonic basis, each triad may be given a dominant seventh quality.

F Major

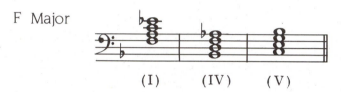

(I)   (IV)   (V)

Play open sevenths that follow this blues progression in F. The Rhythm Cassette will set a rhythmic basis for the sevenths.

I	IV	I	I
IV	IV	I	I
V	IV	I	I

3. Rewind the Rhythm Cassette to 8-3. Choose a partner—one will scat and play melody as the other plays sevenths based on the Rhythm Cassette direction. Use the key of C major.

4. A walking bass is characteristic in blues improvisation. Each harmony change should be started on bass root. Strong bass movement anticipates harmonic change by a step or half step above or below.

5. Rewind the Rhythm Cassette to 8-3. Choose two partners—one will play scat melody, one will play open sevenths, and the third will play walking bass. Use the bass above or create your own.

8

ENSEMBLE

1.

The Silent Lake

from *Duets for Children*, Book 1

SIR WILLIAM WALTON
(1902-1983)

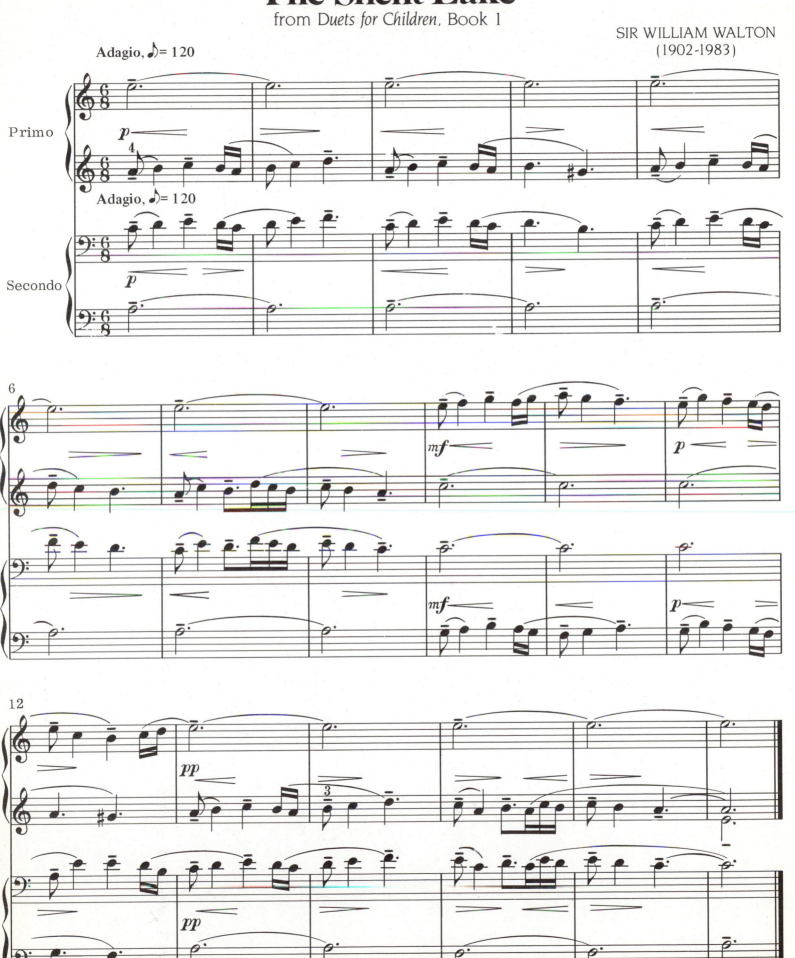

2. Play as written.

Vivace

DANIEL GOTTLOB TÜRK
(1756-1813)

3. Determine the phrases in *Das Morgenrot* (page 178). Divide the four parts among players and perform as an ensemble while conducting.

> Tenor 1 will conduct phrase 1;
> Tenor 2, phrase 2;
> Bass 1, phrase 3;
> Bass 2, phrase 4.

4. As a group, determine dynamics for the Zipoli *Verso*. Individually decide fingering. Play combinations of Parts 1 and 3 and Parts 2 and 3.

Verso

DOMENICO ZIPOLI
(1688-1726)

COMPOSITION

8-4

Using the blues progression from page 186, compose a blues ensemble consisting of bass, chords, and scat melody. Use the keys of F or G major (two choruses with Rhythm Cassette).

SUBSEQUENT REPERTOIRE

Label the form of the *Andantino*.

Andantino†

JOHANN CHRISTIAN BACH/
FRANCESCO PASQUALE RICCI "METHOD"

† Originally untitled   * May be divided between hands

What form of the minor is used in the Lully? Identify points of exact and near imitation.

Menuet

JEAN-BAPTISTE LULLY
(1632-1687)

8

Identify the key relationships in the Haydn.

Gypsy Dance

FRANZ JOSEPH HAYDN, Hob. IX:28/1
(1732-1809)

Analyze the harmony (include inversions) of the *Sonatina* movement.

Sonatina

ALBERT BIEHL
(1835—*ca.* 1899)

9.

Secondary Dominants / Styles of Accompanying

EXEMPLARY REPERTOIRE   **Chorale**, Op. 68, No. 4 Robert Schumann

---

INQUIRY

1. Scan the piece. Observe:

   - chromatically altered chords that function as dominants

     Triads and seventh chords that have been chromatically altered to have the quality of V or V_7 are called *secondary dominants*. They normally resolve to the chords that would serve as their tonics.

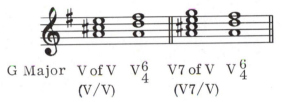

G Major   V of V V_4^6 V7 of V V_4^6
         (V/V)   (V7/V)

   - total harmonic structure
   - connecting pedal

PERFORMANCE

1. Play soprano and bass voices.

2. Play soprano and tenor voices.

3. Play as written.

Chorale
from *Album for the Young*

ROBERT SCHUMANN, Op. 68, No. 4
(1810-1856)

TOPICS TO EXPLORE AND DISCUSS

- *Album for the Young*, Op. 68
- Clara Wieck Schumann
- Transposing Instruments

RELATED SKILLS AND ACTIVITIES

TECHNIQUE

1. Refer to Keyboard Theory Section (page 181). Exercises 1. In the keys of D major, D♭ major, and A major, add left-hand ascending scales. Use traditional fingering.

2. The following is traditional F major/minor scale fingering (2 octaves).

| RH: | 1 | 2 | 3 | 4 | 1 | 2 | 3 | 1 | 2 | 3 | 4 | 1 | 2 | 3 | 4 |
| LH: | 5 | 4 | 3 | 2 | 1 | 3 | 2 | 1 | 4 | 3 | 2 | 1 | 3 | 2 | 1 |

Away from the keyboard on a flat surface, play the scale upward and downward. Say ''1's'' when thumbs play together. Now play on the keyboard, slowly and steadily.

9-1

Play the F major and three forms of F minor scales as directed by the Rhythm Cassette.

3. Rewind the Rhythm Cassette to 8-1 and review the white-key minor scales.

4. Rewind the Rhythm Cassette to 7-1 and review the white-key major scales, and A♭ major.

5. Play the following broken-chord octave extensions.

READING

1. Have one member of the class perform the vocal line.

Soldatenlied

ROBERT SCHUMANN
(1810-1856)

Ein sche - cki - ges Pferd, ein___ blan - kes Ge - wehr und ein

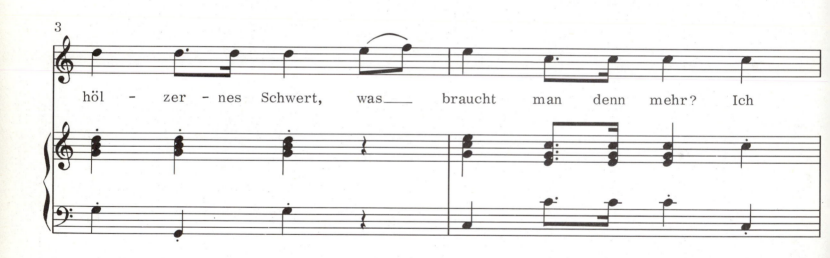

höl - zer - nes Schwert, was___ braucht man denn mehr? Ich

bin ein Sol - dat, man sieht's mir wohl an, ich mar -

schi - re schon grad', halt' Schritt wie ein Mann.

Mit tro - tzi - gem Muth zieh' Mor - gens ich aus, kehr'

freund - lich und gut um Mit - tag nach Haus. So wird ex - er - zirt zum

A - bend noch spat, bis der Schlaf com - man - dirt: zu Bett, Ka - me - rad!

2. Perform Zachau's *Von Himmel hoch* two ways.

- Solo clarinet accompanied by multiple keyboards
- All three parts on keyboards with chorale melody doubled an octave higher

Before playing, decide as a group on appropriate articulation; for example, should all quarter notes be played semidetached?

Von Himmel hoch

FRIEDRICH WILHELM ZACHAU
(1663-1712)
Arranged by Lynn Freeman Olson

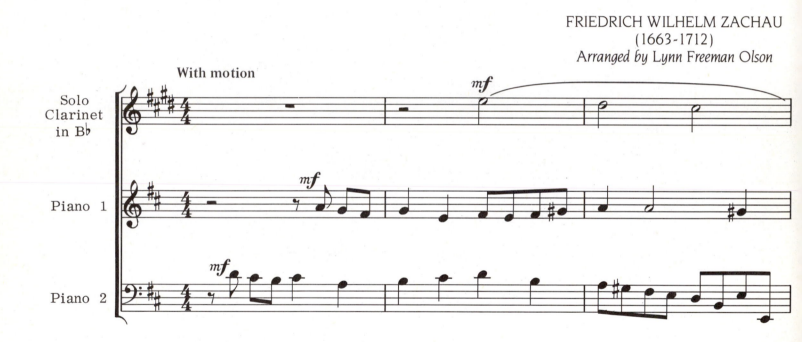

Prelude

GIUSEPPI CONCONE, Op. 37, No.22
(1801-1861)

9

4.

American Tune

Traditional
Arranged by Lynn Freeman Olson

Simply, flowing

mp *legato*

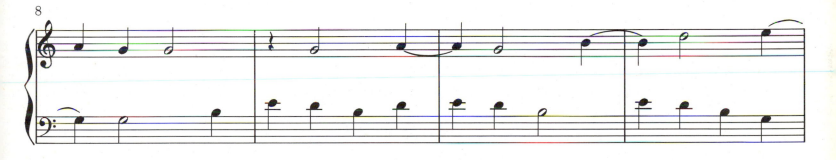

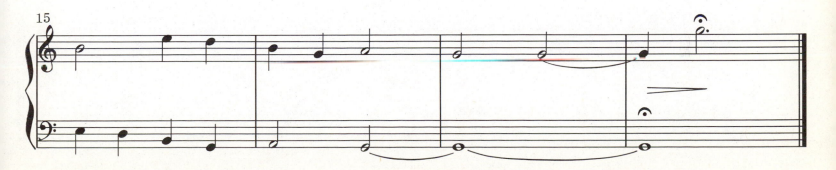

5. Determine chord distribution between right and left hands, and play.

Seelenbräutigam

ADAM DRESE
(1620-1701)

Play the chord of resolution for each secondary dominant. Thinking of **each** key in parentheses as the tonic, analyze and play the secondary dominant and its chord of resolution.

Example:

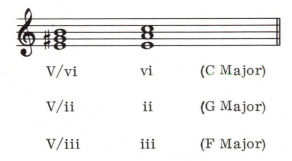

V/vi	vi	(C Major)
V/ii	ii	(G Major)
V/iii	iii	(F Major)

V_5^6/ii	ii	(E♭ Major)
V_5^6/iii	iii	(D♭ Major)
V_5^6/vi	vi	(A♭ Major)

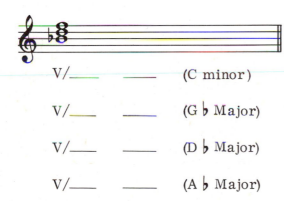

V/___	___	(C minor)
V/___	___	(G♭ Major)
V/___	___	(D♭ Major)
V/___	___	(A♭ Major)

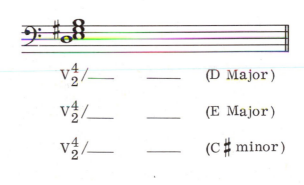

V_2^4/___	___	(D Major)
V_2^4/___	___	(E Major)
V_2^4/___	___	(C♯ minor)

V_3^4/___	___	(B♭ Major)
V_3^4/___	___	(E♭ Major)
V_3^4/___	___	(A♭ Major)
V_3^4/___	___	(F Major)
V_3^4/___	___	(G Major)

HARMONIZATION

1. Develop ostinato patterns that reinforce the AABA form and harmonize the following.

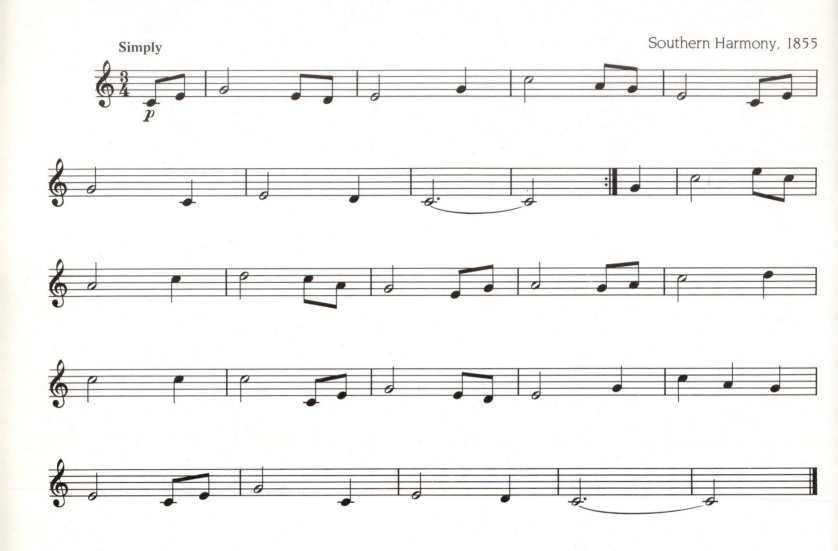

Southern Harmony, 1855

Simply

Transpose to one other pentatonic scale.

2. Harmonize the following melodies, using secondary dominants when appropriate.

THOMAS MORLEY
(1557-1602)

With energy

FRANZ SCHUBERT
(1797-1828)

American

9-2

3. Improvise a two-handed keyboard style accompaniment to the following harmonic changes. The Rhythm Cassette will set the tempo.

$\frac{4}{4}$ | D-7 / G7 / / / | D-7 / G7 / / / | E-7 / A7 / / / | E-7 / A7 / / / | A-7♭5 / D7 / / | A♭-7 / D♭7 / / / |

1. | C / / / / | E-7♭5 / A7 / / / :|| **2.** C / / / / | D-7 / / / | D#°7 / E-7 / / / || G-7 / C7 / / / | G-7 / C7 / / / |

Fmaj7 / / / / | G-7 / C7 / / / | A-7 / D7 / / / | A-7 / D7 / / / | D-7 / G7 / / / | E-7 / A7 / / / || D-7 / G7 / / / |

D-7 / G7 / / / | E-7 / A7 / / / | E-7 / A7 / / / | A-7 / D7 / / / | A♭-7 / D♭7 / / | C / / / / | C / / / / ||

$\frac{4}{4}$ | G G | B B | C C | D D | Em Em | A A | C D | G G |

G G | B B | C C | D D | Em Em | A A | C D | G G ||

G G | G G | C C | C C | A A | A A | D D | D D ||

G G | B B | C C | D D | Em Em | A A | C D | G G ||

4. Complete the harmonization in the three styles indicated.

5. Complete in chorale style.

FELICE DI GIARDINI
(1716-1796)

TRANSPOSITION

1. Transpose the Köhler *Andantino* to D major and A major.

Andantino

LOUIS KOHLER
(1820-1886)

2. Discover as a group why this etude will be easy to transpose. Transpose to at least three other major keys.

Etude

CORNELIUS GURLITT
(1820-1901)

1. The ascending blues scale is formed by adding one note to the blues pentascale—flat 7.

Determine the best fingering and play the F blues scale several times.

Use the 12-bar pattern to play two choruses of blues in F. Accompany with open fifths or sevenths.

I	IV	I	I
IV	IV	I	I
V	IV	I	V (I to end)

2. Rewind the Rhythm Cassette to 9-3 and play right-hand open sevenths or seventh chords with left-hand walking bass in the key of F.

3. Play an "up-tempo" blues improvisation ensemble in F (two choruses with the Rhythm Cassette).

Part 1—blues scale melody   Part 3—open fifths
Part 2—mid-range seventh chords   Part 4—walking bass

Silence is one of the most important aspects of improvisation!

ENSEMBLE

Notturno
(Theme)

FRANZ SCHUBERT, Op. 148
(1797-1828)
Arranged by Lynn Freeman Olson

Lonesome Valley

from *Animated Scale Duets*

Spiritual
Arranged by Dorothy Bishop

Optional Part 3

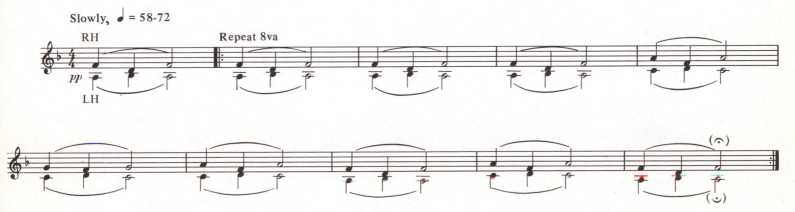

COMPOSITION

Use the following pentatonic scale to create a two-voice composition.

D E F# A B

SUBSEQUENT REPERTOIRE

Locate and analyze resolutions of the secondary dominants used in the *Arietta*.

Arietta

JOHANN CHRISTIAN BACH/
FRANCESCO PASQUALE RICCI "METHOD"

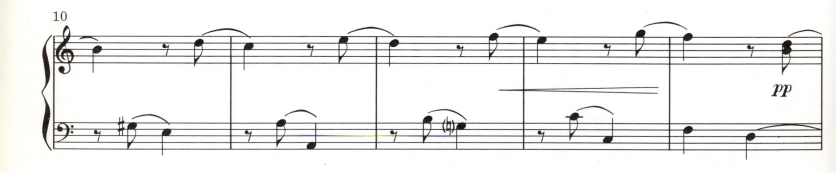

Block each beat of the Mozart *Minuet*. Block each measure containing sixteenths; play other measures as written. Play as written.

Minuet

WOLFGANG AMADEUS MOZART, K. 5
(1756-1791)

Analyze *Prayer* before playing.

Prayer

CORNELIUS GURLITT
(1820-1901)

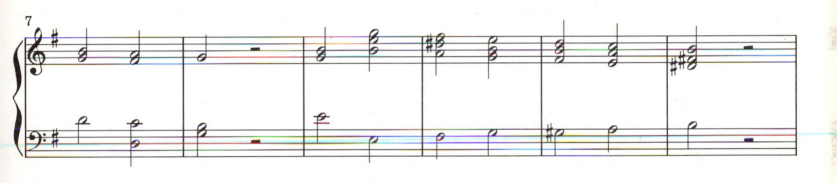

In the Graham, block chord shapes before playing.

In Soft Winter Rain

from *At Lake Nojiri in Japan*

ROBERT GRAHAM

10.

Melodic Ornamentation

EXEMPLARY REPERTOIRE   **Minuet** Johann Krieger

INQUIRY

1. Scan the piece. Observe:

   • sequence
   • movement of voices
   • articulation plan

2. Discuss phrasing and how it will be influenced by articulation.

PERFORMANCE

1. Play the lower voice only, paying particular attention to fingering.

2. Play as written.

3. It was a fairly common performance practice in eighteenth century music to vary recurring materials by adding figuration to the written score. In addition to increased ornamentation of the trill and mordent variety, it was natural for the performer to "fill in" tones, especially in the small skips. On a repeat, for example:

Rhythmic variations were common also. A single held chord or tone could be given new vigor through repetition,

and "straight" rhythms could be "bent" to provide a new buoyancy. In many cases, these dotted rhythms were played in a "lazy" or rounded manner when a gentle lilt was appropriate.

Following the original version of the Krieger *Minuet*, we have suggested some ways to ornament the patterns. Use these ideas and vary them. This practice is called "melodic ornamentation" and, as in all such matters, your own sense of style and taste should be your main guide.

Minuet

JOHANN KRIEGER
(1651-1738)

Possible melodic ornamentation:

TOPICS TO EXPLORE AND DISCUSS

- Johann Krieger
- Musical impetus for melodic ornamentation

RELATED SKILLS AND ACTIVITIES

TECHNIQUE

1. The following are traditional fingerings for E♭ major and D♭ major scales (two octaves).
   Note the left hand.

E♭ Major:	RH: 3	1	2	3	4	1	2	3	1	2	3	4	1	2	3
	LH: 3	2	1	4	3	2	1	3	2	1	4	3	2	1	3

B♭ Major:	RH: 4	1	2	3	1	2	3	4	1	2	3	1	2	3	4
	LH: 3	2	1	4	3	2	1	3	2	1	4	3	2	1	2

10-1

Away from the keyboard on a flat surface, play the scales upward and downward. Now play on the keyboard, slowly and steadily. Play the scales as directed by the Rhythm Cassette.

2. Rewind the Rhythm Cassette to 9-1 and review the F major/minor scales on page 200.

READING

1.

Wiegenlied

WOLFGANG AMADEUS MOZART
(1756-1791)

Schlafe, mein Prinzchen, schlaf ein, es ruhn nun Schäfchen und Vö - ge - lein,

Gar - ten und Wie - se ver - stummt, auch nicht ein Bienchen mehr summt,

Lu - na mit sil - ber - nem Schein guc - ket zum Fen - ster her - ein,

schlafe bei sil - ber-nem Schein,   schlafe, mein Prinzchen, schlaf ein,   schlaf

ein, _____ schlaf ein!

2. Bring out the top line in *Bed Time*.

Bed Time

from *Pieces for the Young Pianist*, Vol. 2

ALEC WILDER
(1907-1983)

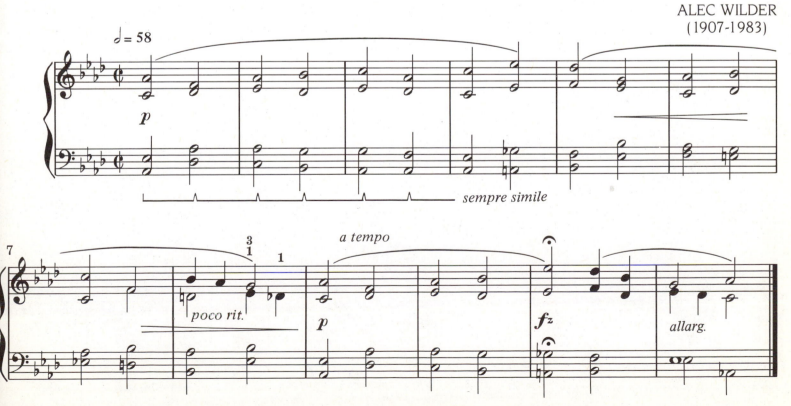

3. Play the accompaniment as a partner plays the violin line.

Sonata in D Major
for Violin and Piano (excerpt)

FRANZ SCHUBERT, Op. posth. 137, No. 1
(1797-1828)

4. Play Humperdinck's *Children's Prayer* using right hand only.

Children's Prayer
from the Opera *Hansel and Gretel*

ENGELBERT HUMPERDINCK
(1854-1921)
Arranged by Lynn Freeman Olson

5. Play several paired parts in the Brahms.

Abschiedslied
from *Deutsche Volkslieder*

JOHANNES BRAHMS
(1833-1897)

KEYBOARD THEORY

1. Play the following progressions as directed by the Rhythm Cassette. There will be a rewind for new keys.

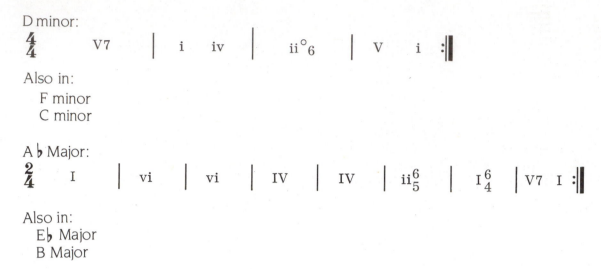

D minor:

$\frac{4}{4}$ V7 | i iv | ii°6 | V i :||

Also in:
F minor
C minor

A♭ Major:

$\frac{2}{4}$ I | vi | vi | IV | IV | ii$^6_5$ | I$^6_4$ | V7 I :||

Also in:
E♭ Major
B Major

2. Play this progression with Rhythm Cassette background. Use two-handed accompaniment style. Rewind for new keys.

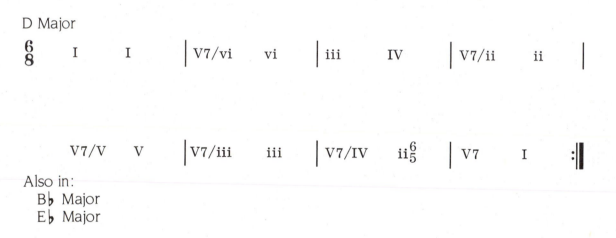

D Major

$\frac{6}{8}$ I I | V7/vi vi | iii IV | V7/ii ii |

V7/V V | V7/iii iii | V7/IV ii$^6_5$ | V7 I :||

Also in:
B♭ Major
E♭ Major

HARMONIZATION

1. Furnish a bass line for the Humperdinck on page 236 and play hands together.

2. Harmonize with the chords given.

British

Dreamily

p I   IV   I   V7 of V   V

V7   I$^6_4$ V7   I$^6_4$ V   I   IV

I$^6_4$ V7 I   V7   I   V7   I   V7 of V   V7   I

10

PETER ILYICH TCHAIKOVSKY
(1840-1893)

Andantino

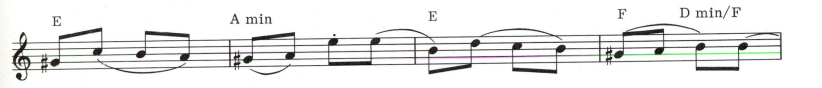

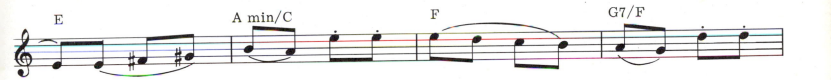

3. Harmonize.

Scottish

Not fast

4. Complete in the style indicated.

Czechoslovakian

Happily

etc.

IV   I6   ii V_5^6 of ii

ii   V7 I_4^6 V_5^6 V7   I

AMILCARE PONCHIELLI
(1834-1886)

TRANSPOSITION

1. Transpose to
   - Parallel Dorian
   - Parallel Phrygian
   - A Major

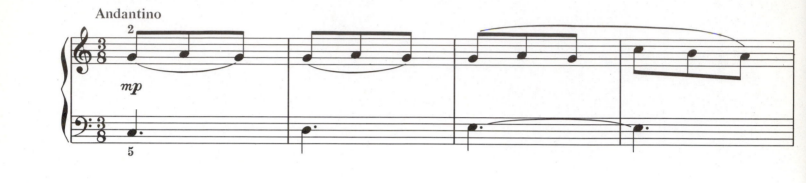

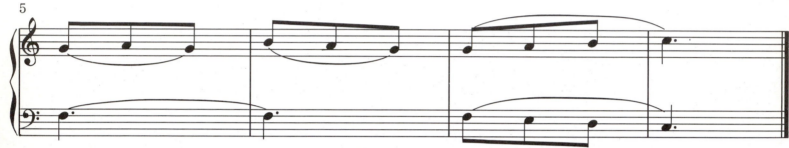

2. Transpose to begin on C.

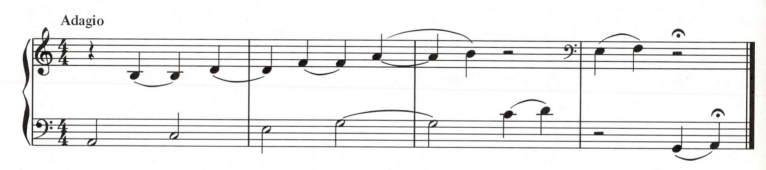

IMPROVISATION

1. Improvise a two-handed accompaniment appropriate for each basic movement.

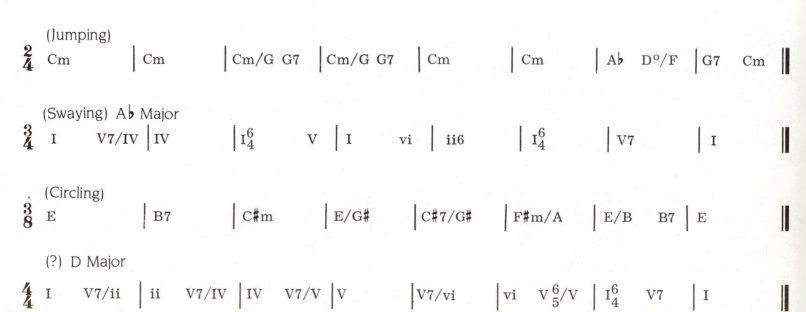

2. Improvise three choruses of blues in F:

- First 12 bars—walking bass and harmony (fifths or sevenths)
- Second 12 bars—harmony and melody (use some scat)
- Third 12 bars—walking bass and harmony

Use V as the turnaround harmony at the end of the first and second chorus. The Rhythm Cassette will set the tempo.

10-4

ENSEMBLE

The Hunt
from *Seven Piece Suite for Piano Duet*

ELSIE WELLS

From: *Seven Piece Suite for Piano Duet* by Elsie Wells (1979). By permission of Oxford University Press.

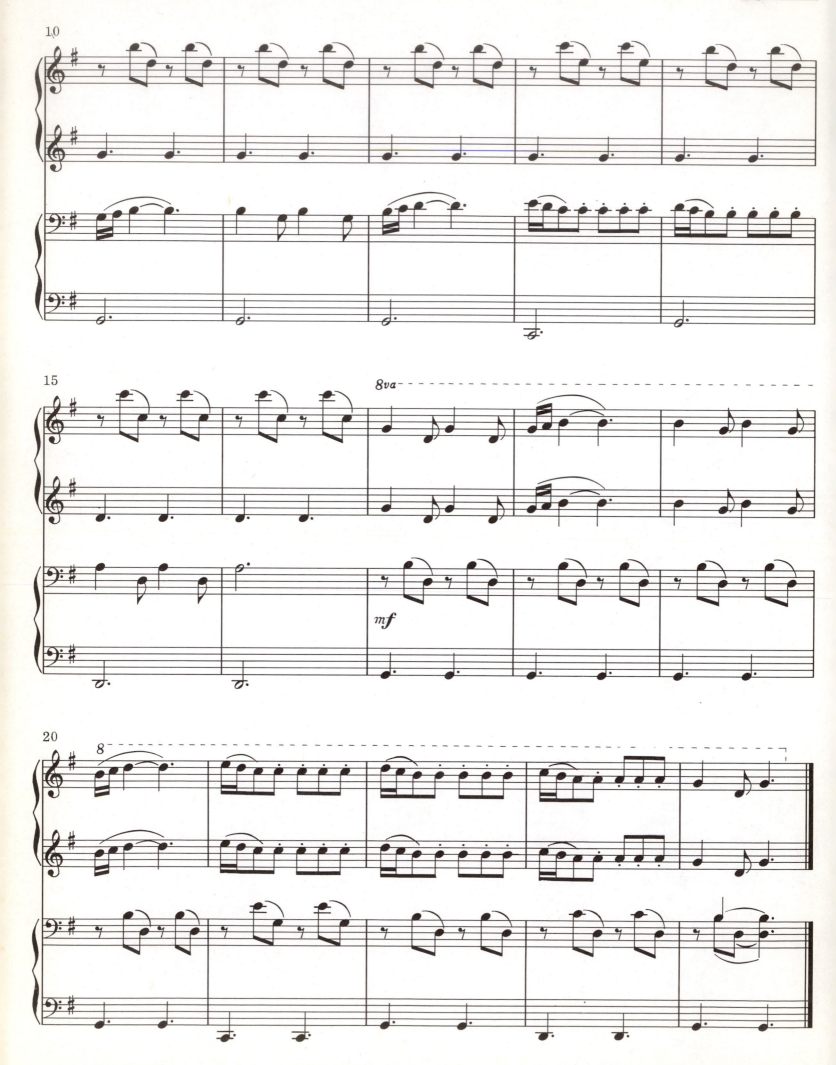

American Ballad
from 4 × 4

JENÖ TAKACS

* Original pedal indications for one acoustic piano. When performed on separate pianos. Primo may pedal in a simiar manner.

COMPOSITION

Compose a minuet in eighteenth century style suitable for melodic ornamentation - 16 bar, binary.
Use the following rhythmic motive.

SUBSEQUENT REPERTOIRE

Use melodic ornamentation on repeats in the Telemann *Fantasie*.

Fantasie
(excerpt)

GEORG PHILIPP TELEMANN
(1681-1764)

*⌢ only at Fine

D.C. al ⌢ (with repeat)

Play the *Waltz* without pedal.

Waltz
from *24 Pieces for Children*

DMITRI KABALEVSKY, Op. 39, No. 13
(1904-   )

Determine logical fingering for the Haydn.

German Dance

FRANZ JOSEPH HAYDN
(1732-1809)

White Lily

from *For Children*, Vol. 1

BELA BARTÓK
(1881-1945)

Observe ties in the Bartók.

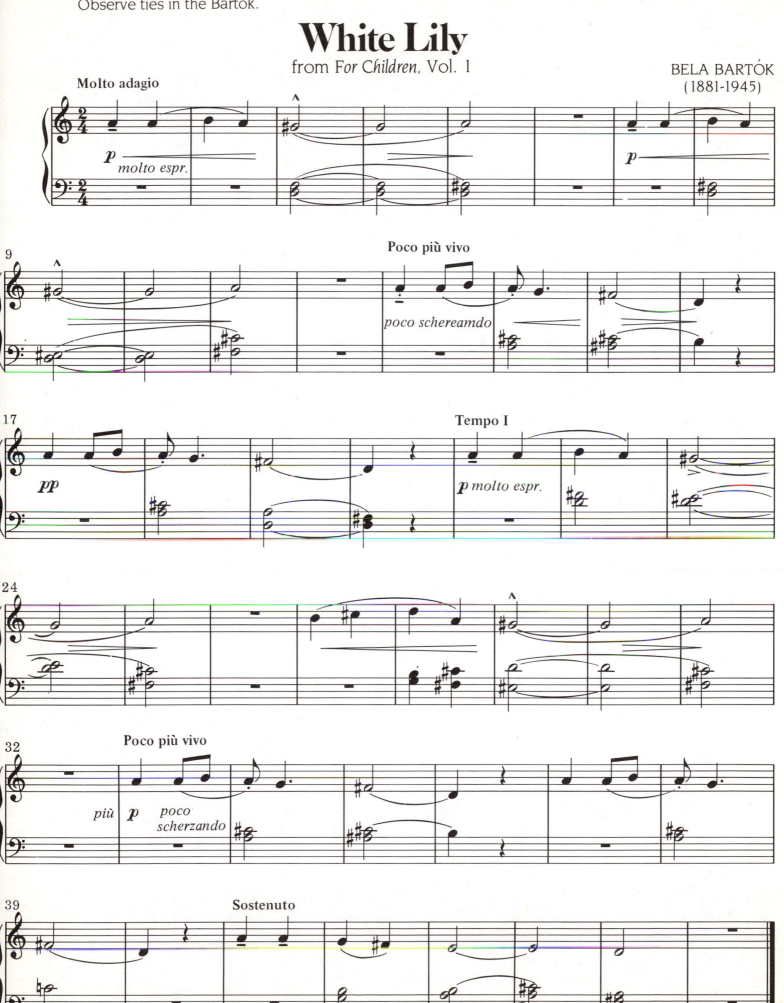

Observe articulation in *The Chase*.

The Chase

FRIEDRICH BURGMÜLLER, Op. 100, No. 9
(1806-1874)

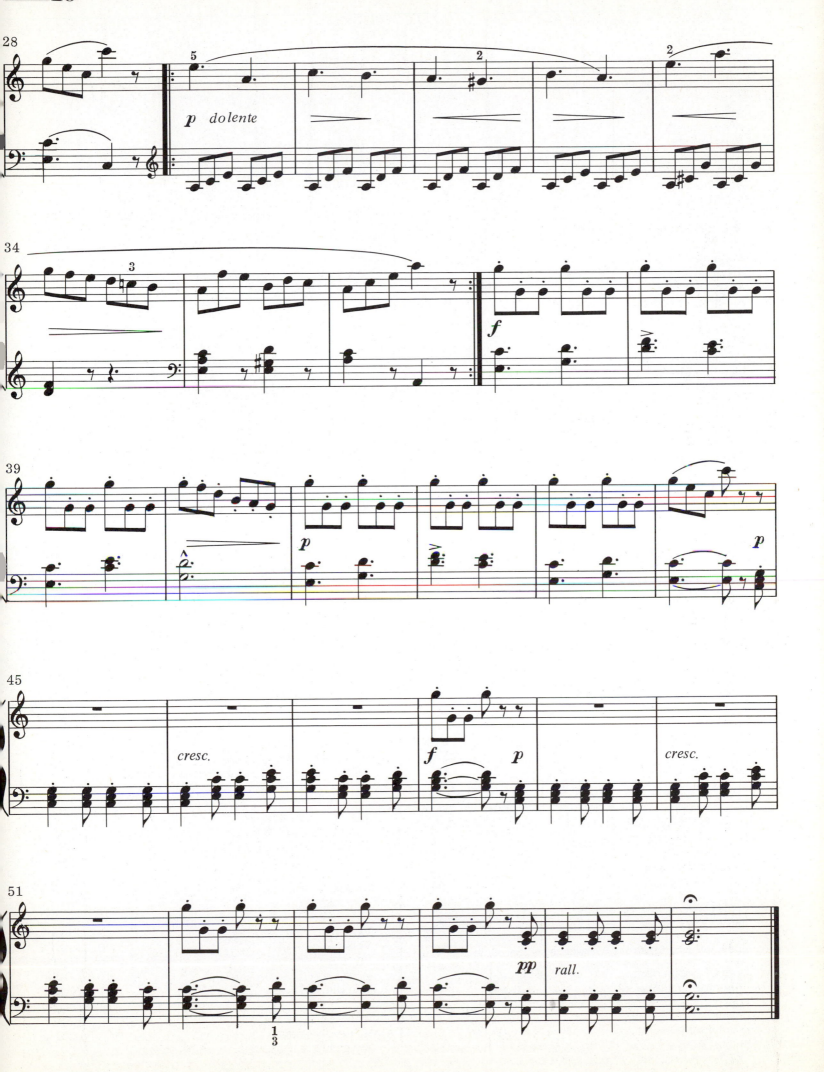

Index of Titles

Index of Composers

Index of Composers